"*Bread of Life* gave me the tools and motivation to get my hands covered in flour and my family feasting on fresh-baked bread. But Abigail's words go far beyond baking—she compels me to eat and enjoy the bread of life himself. This book is for women who are hungry for something this world hasn't been able to provide—who want to cultivate an appetite that can taste the Lord's goodness without an undertone of cynicism, scoffing, and suspicion. I'm so grateful for the words of this sage older sister in Christ."

Emily Jensen, coauthor, *Risen Motherhood: Gospel Hope for Everyday Moments*; cofounder, Risen Motherhood

"If you're into making bread, this book is definitely for you. If you aspire to be a bread baker, this book will help you get started. And if, like me at this season of my life, it's highly doubtful that you will ever make bread, you will still be inspired by this book. Wherever you fall on that spectrum, you'll find the pictures and descriptions of freshly made bread tantalizing. And best of all, Abigail's devotional meditations will make you hungry for more of Jesus, the bread of life."

Nancy DeMoss Wolgemuth, Founder, *Revive our Hearts*; Host, *Revive Our Hearts*

"I admit I know almost nothing about making bread. In fact, since being diagnosed with celiac disease years ago, I don't eat any bread (I mean delicious bread with gluten in it!). But I do know good writing and good thinking when I see it, and both are here in Abigail's book. Her devotional meditations are thoughtful, engaging, biblical, and wise. And maybe even better for you than gluten."

Kevin DeYoung, Senior Pastor, Christ Covenant Church, Matthews, North Carolina; Assistant Professor of Systematic Theology, Reformed Theological Seminary, Charlotte

"In the midst of our daily need for sustenance, Abigail delightfully and tenderly calls our hungry souls to what truly satisfies."

Ruth Chou Simons, author, *Beholding and Becoming* and *GraceLaced*; artist; Founder, GraceLaced Co.

"God has used his word to show me the beauty in the ordinary work I do to serve my family. He has also used the journey of baking bread to show me more of the beauty of the gospel and his kingdom. It is ordinary work, but it is also extraordinary. What is there that is like it? Matthew 13:33 tells us that God's kingdom is like leaven that a woman hid in flour. Ordinary things, ordinary work, ordinary food, ordinary faithfulness—they all work together to accomplish glorious things. This book is a lovely reflection on this rich intersection of the ordinary and the glorious. I hope it inspires many women!"

Rachel Jankovic, author, *You Who?* and *Loving the Little Years*

"This book is such a lovely reminder that God's word speaks truth and that his world also speaks truth. The physical gift of baking does more than sustain us physically and give us great pleasure—it tells us something about our own sweet Savior, Jesus. The spiritual metaphors of baking are many, and Abigail calls them up masterfully, one by one. It's so rare to find a book that is both physically beautiful and theologically weighty. In her prose, Abigail brings us something true, deep, and lovely to sink our teeth into. But in her recipes, she's given us something worthwhile to sink our hands into. What a gift. This book will end up blessing my whole family."

Tilly Dillehay, author, *Seeing Green* and *Broken Bread*; cohost, *Home Fires* podcast

BREAD OF LIFE

BREAD OF LIFE

SAVORING THE ALL-SATISFYING GOODNESS OF JESUS
THROUGH THE ART OF BREAD MAKING

A B I G A I L D O D D S

WHEATON, ILLINOIS

Library of Congress Cataloging-in-Publication Data
Names: Dodds, Abigail, 1981– author.
Title: Bread of life : savoring the all-satisfying goodness of Jesus through the art of bread making / Abigail Dodds.
Description: Wheaton, Illinois : Crossway, 2021. | Includes bibliographical references and index.
Identifiers: LCCN 2020051480 (print) | LCCN 2020051481 (ebook) | ISBN 9781433572470 (hardcover) | ISBN 9781433572487 (pdf) | ISBN 9781433572494 (mobi) | ISBN 9781433572500 (epub)
Subjects: LCSH: Food--Religious aspects—Christianity. | Bread—Religious aspects—Christianity. | Cooking (Bread)
Classification: LCC BR115.N87 D63 2021 (print) | LCC BR115.N87 (ebook) | DDC 248—dc23
LC record available at https://lccn.loc.gov/2020051480
LC ebook record available at https://lccn.loc.gov/2020051481

And he who sits on the throne will shelter them with his presence.
They shall hunger no more, neither
thirst anymore.

REVELATION 7:15–16

For my pastor, John Piper,
whose hunger for God has fed me over and over again.

And for my family,
who helped me see the glory of bread by their enthusiasm for eating it.
Let's keep eating together—the bread and the Bread.

CONTENTS

Introduction

This is an unusual book. It's a book, written to women, that is *primarily spiritual* yet has recipes in it. It's not a self-help book. It's not a diet book. It is a book about hunger, bread, the word of God, and Jesus.

I thought it would be fitting to include bread recipes since we'll be talking about bread so much, but it's also a way to help you understand some of what the Bible says about bread in a concrete, hands-on way. Consider the recipes your Sunday school flannel graph, your show and tell. The other benefit of including bread recipes is that you'll have something very tangible to do when you're done reading that actually blesses people and may move you along in obeying God. It's one way to get busy at home, in your kitchen, for the good of your people and your neighbors and anybody who would be blessed by a fresh loaf. Making bread is just one of a million little things that you could do to serve and obey God, to love others, and to delight in God's good gifts.

A PRACTICAL NOTE ABOUT THOSE RECIPES AND WHAT YOU NEED TO GET STARTED

You may wonder from whence my recipes have come! I don't claim any real originality, although some of the recipes have sort of become my own over time. Each recipe has a source that you can find in the footnotes, even if my version of it isn't all that similar to the source any longer.

You'll notice there are no gluten-free recipes. There is nothing intentional behind this; simply my finitude. I love my gluten-free friends and recognize that some of them can't come near the stuff because of celiac disease or severe sensitivities. As someone who has never made gluten-free bread (I have made gluten-free meals), I figured that those desiring to learn how would be better served by the gluten-free experts. Rather than try to give you something I've never done before, I simply encourage you to seek out great gluten-free recipes online or from friends.

Furthermore, you may wonder why two of the recipes (Sourdough Country Loaf and Chocolate Croissants) give measurements in grams first, then measurements in cups in the parentheses, when the rest give measurements in cups first, then the measurements in grams in parentheses. This is because those two recipes are more exacting than the others, so it would be a real benefit to you if you had a kitchen scale in addition to measuring cups so that you can weigh your ingredients for the best results.[1] In light of the kitchen scale recommendation, I thought it might be helpful to make a list of the things you'll need on hand if you've never made bread before.

FLOUR, WATER, SALT, YEAST

Flour, water, salt, and yeast make up the basic ingredients of bread. Of course, there are plenty of recipes in this book for which you will need other ingredients, such as butter, oil, chocolate, sugar, eggs, milk, and cheese. But for basic bread, that's what you'll need. I recommend that you start buying unbleached all-purpose flour, as that is the most versatile flour for all kinds of recipes. Sometimes you'll need a different kind of flour like bread flour or wheat flour, but usually the recipe calls for unbleached all-purpose flour.

A BIG BOWL AND A LARGE SPOON

So very complicated, isn't it? But seriously, you need a big bowl and a large spoon. Only one of the recipes in this book requires an electric stand mixer. The rest are mixed by hand in a big bowl with a large, sturdy spoon (or occasionally a whisk). I usually use something called a "Danish dough hook" to mix my dough, which is my version of a large spoon, but you could use a wooden spoon or rubber spatula. Other tools such as a bench scraper or a bread lame are helpful, but you can get by without them. You can't get by without a big bowl and a large mixing spoon.

AN OVEN

You thought this would be a tricky list, didn't you? Nope. You need an oven, preferably one that heats up to 500 degrees.

BAKING DISHES

Different breads bake in different dishes. A Dutch oven with a lid or a cast iron pot with a lid will be needed for some. Loaf pans, baking sheets, muffin tins, and a 9x13

pan are all used at one time or another in these recipes. For sourdough, it's helpful to have proofing baskets, but regular bowls lined with tea towels are an easy substitution.

PARCHMENT PAPER

You will find that parchment paper shows up all the time! You can buy some at the store. In some cases, a silicon baking mat will work fine as a substitute, but other times you really just need the parchment paper.

A KITCHEN SCALE

As I mentioned above, a few of these recipes require a kitchen scale. The reason is that when we measure flour, it is easy to get our measurements off. Some presift their flour by fluffing it up with a spoon so that it's not densely packed down before measuring in the cup; some don't. A scale takes all the guess work out and gives you much more consistent results in your baking. If baking becomes a regular thing for you, you'll definitely want a kitchen scale.

Whether you've never made bread before or you already love to make bread, I think you'll find that these eleven recipes will take you from zero to one hundred and everywhere in between. Most of the recipes make two loaves, so take that as a good excuse to give one away!

TWO OTHER ABSOLUTE ESSENTIALS

Now that we've been over what you need to get started baking, I want to remind you that there are only two things you need to get started with *spiritual bread*, and I could even make the case for only one thing. The one thing is the Bible. You need God's word because that's where you'll find the bread—Jesus. The second thing is God's people. That's it. You don't need colorful highlighters or a formal book study or fancy Bible software or a pretty prayer journal—as nice as those things may be. You need the book and you need the people of the book. God's Spirit works through his word and through his people. If you've got those, you've got what's essential.

I hope you enjoy this niche genre of biblical-theological-written-for-women-all-about-Jesus-bread-making book. If you're reading, I want you to know you've been prayed for—by me and others who care about the outcome of your faith. What deep hopes and desires I have for you, dear reader! I'd like to take a moment and pray for all of us:

Father,

Whatever it takes, have your way in us. Give us a holy hatred for our sin. Forgive us by the blood of your Son for the ways we've sinned against you. Nourish us with the bread of your Son and grant to us to live forever with you in the age to come. Give us the faith of children as we walk on this earth and the joy of eating your word every day. Make us happy, thankful, holy women who hope in God, even when we are persecuted or sick or sorrowful. Be glorified in us, we pray.

In Jesus's name, Amen.

I hope you add your amen to that prayer. It has been a ridiculous amount of fun and a great privilege to put this book together for you.

Savor the words as you enjoy the recipes.

1

Why This Book Has Nothing and Everything to Do with Your Diet

Your words were found, and I ate them,
and your words became to me a joy
and the delight of my heart,
for I am called by your name,
O Lord, God of hosts.

JEREMIAH 15:16

So, whether you eat or drink, or whatever you do,
do all to the glory of God.

1 CORINTHIANS 10:31

T he goal of this book is to change your diet. I want you to start eating bread. Every day. Without moderation. I want you awash in gluten—but not the gluten you buy at the store or eat in your kitchen.

I'm not asking you to follow some new gluten-only fad or to research ancient grains or to buy into a method of slow food or fast food. The goal of this book is to awaken your appetite for a different kind of diet—a spiritual diet—that consists of the bread of life, the Lord Jesus revealed in the Bible.

When Satan tempted Jesus in the wilderness, the first thing he did was appeal to Jesus's real and basic need for physical food. "Then Jesus was led up by the Spirit into the wilderness to be tempted by the devil. And after fasting forty days and forty nights, he was hungry. And the tempter came and said to him, 'If you are the Son of God, command these stones to become loaves of bread'" (Matt. 4:1–3).

Eating isn't sinful, except when it is. Jesus knew this. Eating physical food is part of how God has made us. It isn't sinful to eat. But it is sinful to use physical food as a substitute for spiritual food, in the same way that it is sinful to put *anything* in the place of God. That's what Satan was trying to get Jesus to do in the wilderness, which is why Jesus answers Satan like this: "It is written, 'Man shall not live by bread alone, but by every word that comes from the mouth of God'" (Matt. 4:4).

THE SPIRITUAL AFFECTS THE PHYSICAL AND VICE VERSA

Our spiritual diet takes precedence over our physical diet. Not only that, but our spiritual diet rules and reigns over our physical diet—not as a tyrant and taskmaster, making us obsessive control freaks about what goes into our mouth, but as a gratitude-producing, Christ-honoring governor. Our physical diets bow the knee to Jesus because he is the bread of life, who has taught us what true satisfaction is. What we consume spiritually affects all of our life, whether our thoughts, our words, or our actions.

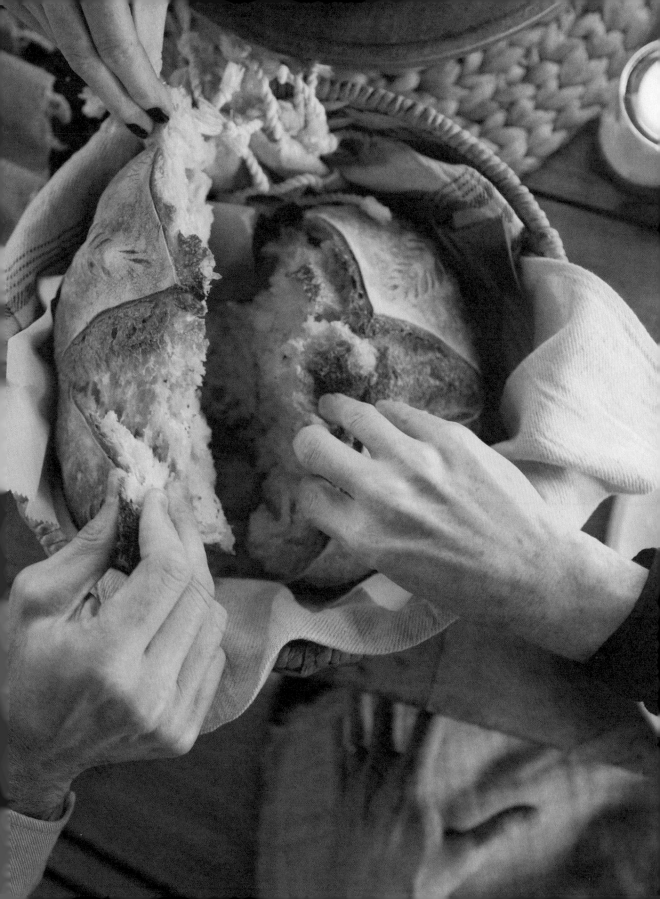

When Jesus answers the tempter in the wilderness by appealing to God's words as his food, he is reminding all of us what our true provision actually is (Matt. 4:1–4)! What is our food? God's words. And who is the Word of God made flesh? The man, Jesus, God's Son.

The goal of this book is to make that Word, the Lord Jesus, who is revealed on every page of the Scriptures, the substance of your spiritual diet. What does that have to do with your physical diet? Nothing! And everything. I'm not here to tell you what you ought to eat for breakfast, lunch, or supper. I have some fun recipes to share, but those will only do you good if you can wield them by faith, in service and with gratitude, not as part of a diet plan! But I do believe all the way to my innards that when we start to be nourished by Christ in God's word, it changes everything about us. No part of our lives goes untouched. Jesus razes and remakes the whole shebang, including simple things like breakfast, lunch, and dinner. He may or may not change your menu. Taco Tuesday will hopefully endure, but he will change the heart that cooks the beef and shreds the chicken and consumes the salsa. And that heart will be a grateful heart that can eat what is placed in front of it to the glory of God (1 Cor. 10:31).

Too often we seek solutions to our sin problems by getting a little myopic on what tools are at our disposal. As I've been bent over and sweating in my garden lately, I'm reminded that weeds are persistent. I'm also reminded that, to switch from metaphor to cliché, there is more than one way to skin a cat. Clear as mud?

DRENCHING THE WEEDS RATHER THAN PULLING THEM

There is more than one way to kill the weeds of sin, but the thing all weed killing has in common is that it is empowered by the Spirit of God, who speaks through the word of God. Sometimes we are trying desperately to pull up a weed from the roots. But the ground is dry, the weed is stubborn, and we just keep ending up with a handful of leaves while the roots remain underneath. What if we tried something new? What if we stepped back and sprayed them with weed killer? What if we put a tarp over them until they suffocated? What if we got out the rototiller and went to town?

I think when it comes to food-related sins such as gluttony or asceticism, we often fixate on the physical food itself.[2] Counting calories and obsessing over ingredient lists and spending all our time on the physical food is not the same thing as killing the sin of gluttony or asceticism. It's a bit like pulling on a stubborn weed when the ground is bone dry and the roots are deep and ending up falling backward with a fistful of stem and leaves. In some cases, the obsessing over the food is actually putting fertilizer on the weeds while you trim back a few leaves with a scissors. You might think you're killing them, when in fact, even as the diet may produce some results of weight loss or gain, the weed of gluttony or asceticism has doubled in size.

What if you tried something else? What if you stopped tugging on the weed and started dousing it with the word of God? What if you drenched it in the truth? As you are tempted to relieve boredom or to distract from work or to comfort stress or to give yourself a feeling of control by food, what might happen if, rather than just tell yourself to *"Quit it! Stop doing that!"* you satisfied yourself with a better food, God's word? What if you followed Jesus's example and ate the word right in the midst of the temptation—opening up your Bible or your Bible app and confronting yourself and your temptation to sin? What if you prayed those potent words back to God and asked him for help in your time of need? I suspect the temptation would shrivel up and die, because the word of God inhabits more than one metaphor! It's not only bread to nourish us; it's also a

sword for killing, as Ephesians 6 and Hebrews 4 remind us (or in this instance, less of a sword and more like weed poison).[3]

In dousing the sin of gluttony or asceticism in the truth, we are shifting our gaze away from the sin itself and onto what really satisfies: the word of the Lord. At first glance this may not seem like dealing with the problem head-on because we aren't addressing your past or the possible reasons behind the impulse to sinfully use food, but let's face it: we rarely are able to fully understand ourselves or why we do what we do. God's word provides a lasting solution because it can slowly untangle the reasons, even as it helps us shift our attention to what's better. So instead of waiting for the weed to succumb to our tugging, instead of believing that we'll be right with God once those pounds come off, or once our home is well-ordered, or once we've established a great prayer routine, or once we've dug through all the problems of our past, we can take up his word as our weapon of offense—our hose of godly, weed-killing poison—and be right with him now.

BEGIN WHERE YOU ARE

We must not try to *finish* something when we're actually just beginning. We also must not try to begin as *someone other* than ourselves. And we must not try to begin *where* we aren't actually located. Each of us comes to this book at a different starting point and as a unique person.[4] If we're always seeking to make progress as the person we wish we were on our good days, or from the place we think we might be in five years, or where we were six months ago, we will never truly begin. So, I ask you, in the words of C. S. Lewis, to "begin where you are."[5]

We can be right with God this instant, no matter how totally dried up our appetite is for God and the Bible, no matter how out of hand the envy and bitterness have become, no matter how much apathy has infected our soul but we're pretending doesn't exist, no matter how out of whack our current physical diet may be, or how embarrassingly large any outward or inward sin may have grown. I invite you to go to the Lord now, to confess and repent of the sins that you're aware of, and to begin where you are. You can begin to wield his word in this battle—both as the food that truly satisfies and the weapon by which we kill sin.

Discussion Questions

1. What is your spiritual diet like right now?

2. What would it look like for you to start wielding the word of God in the battle against sin?

3. How can you begin where you are rather than stalling out because you wish you were further along from the start? What other Christian can you link arms with as you begin?

ARTISAN BREAD FOR BEGINNERS

Note that this is an overnight recipe.[6] If you want low-risk high-reward bread, this is it. This isn't too hard! Try it!

6½ cups (884 grams)
of unbleached
all-purpose flour

1 teaspoon (3 grams)
instant yeast

1 tablespoon
(17 grams) salt

3 cups (708 grams) water

makes two loaves

Variations: You can turn these loaves into all sorts of wonderful variations: add parmesan and thyme; or feta and sun-dried tomatoes; or rosemary, parmesan, and kalamata olives. For a sweet version, add chocolate chips! Those ingredients can be folded into the loaves right after you've divided the dough in two pieces. If you're wondering how much to add, eyeball it. That's what I do.

THE EVENING BEFORE BAKING:

Whisk the flour, yeast, and salt in a large mixing bowl.

Add the water and mix until a dough is formed. It might look shaggy.

Cover the bowl and let it sit on the counter for 12–18 hours (overnight).

ON BAKING DAY:

Put a Dutch oven or a cast iron pot with lid in the oven and preheat to 500 degrees. (If you have two Dutch ovens, you can put both in the oven and make two loaves at the same time; otherwise you can bake them consecutively.)

Turn the dough out onto a floured counter; divide it in two pieces with a bench scraper or knife. Shape each piece into a round loaf (the dough is sticky, so make sure your hands are floured and simply fold the dough onto itself as best you can—don't worry if it looks messy).

Transfer the loaves to heavily floured parchment paper.

Let the loaves sit until oven is fully preheated.

Pick up the parchment paper with the dough on it and place it in the Dutch oven. Cover it with the lid.

Turn the oven down to 450 degrees and bake for 30 minutes.

Remove the lid and bake for another 15 minutes.

Remove the bread from the pot and cool it on a cooling rack.

2

From Scoffer to Baker

How long will scoffers delight in their scoffing
and fools hate knowledge?

PROVERBS 1:22

A wise son hears his father's instruction,
but a scoffer does not listen to rebuke.

PROVERBS 13:1

D o you remember 2010—that fateful year when Pinterest first hit the interwebs, just a short two and a half years after the iPhone invaded the market and smartphones began to overtake every facet of life? I remember hearing about how you could save a webpage in a folder with the click of a button so you could easily come back to it later. Pin it. Pretty soon I had an account, and I was pinning away—articles, knitting projects, kids' activities, and the occasional recipe. I remember when I first came across a picture of a beautiful round loaf of bread.

My experience with bread didn't go far beyond the bread aisle at the grocery store. My only contact with homemade bread was when my mom got a bread machine when I was middle-school aged. I liked the bread just fine, but I loved the smell. I remember staring in at the top, watching the dough go round and round. When the bread machine phase wore off, we went back to store-bought bread, and that was that.

When I met my would-be husband, one of the standout things about his mother was her cooking (not unlike my mom). She also happened to be a regular bread maker. I was generally intimidated by that, among other things: she was from the big city; I was from a small town in Iowa. She'd been honing her culinary skills for decades; I was twenty-one years old and had perfected one cookie recipe.

Once I was married, I became a permanent resident in the big city, just like my mother-in-law. My husband and I found a church to call home, and I started to get to know the strangers who were my brothers and sisters in Christ. It was then that I began occasionally hearing of other women besides my mother-in-law who made their own bread. It always seemed like the kind of thing that was said *about* someone, to let you know just what sort of woman she was: "Oh, Betsy, yes. Did you know she makes her own bread?" Almost certainly to be followed by, "And churns butter on the back porch too!" or, "And darns all their socks by hand!" or, "She even grinds the wheat in her own mill!" or, "She grows all their food in her garden!" And, naturally, the most obvious follow-up: "She homeschools their ten children."

These sorts of women were more legend to me than anything else. The kind of legend I was quick to scoff at in the privacy of my own head. *Don't you know you can buy bread? Are they just trying to be better than everyone else?* Or the ever charitable, *They must have a lot of time on their hands!*

SHEDDING CYNICISM LIKE HORSE HAIR IN LATE JUNE

Two years after Pinterest came on the scene, this scoffer was finally giving way to something else. "Something else" because I wouldn't call myself a baker at that point—more like a one-off wing-it success story, which is still something. That picture of the beautiful round loaf had worked on me for a while. My cynicism—under the spell of gorgeous photography and endless possibilities—was shedding the way chunks of thick hair start falling off of horses after a long Midwest winter when the temps finally heat up in late June. I pored over bread recipes like they were a Sherlock Holmes novel. I read carefully so as to not miss any important clues and as quickly as my brain would allow so as to unlock the great mystery at the end.

I didn't even know where to buy yeast—what aisle would it be in? Bread aisle? Baking aisle? Refrigerator section? What does it even look like? Is it liquid or solid? Eventually, I found both active yeast and instant yeast, which confused me greatly, so I bought them both. At that stage of life, I had four young children, so their enthusiasm spurred me on when my inner scoffer started to chide. When we pulled those very first round loaves out of our oven, their whole bodies pulsed with aroma-infused delight.

I knew this was something I'd be doing for years to come. The terrific dread of attempting something beyond my skill set became addicting in the best way. The failures were frequent but only ever fuel to keep going. We were being stuffed full of memories and gluten. My children were eating homemade bread—and what was wonderful about it was not mainly the nutritional benefits but that they were eating tangible love from their mom. That's what I've been aiming at ever since. And that's why this book has bread recipes in it—because it's part of how God helped me learn the enjoyment of good works and the benefits of simple things done with love in the name of Jesus and for his glory. I hope the recipes are a means to that end in your life.

Since 2012, I've grown as a baker and home cook. There's always a thousand miles more to go, but that's part of the fun of the whole thing. What is much more notable is that this growth in baking corresponded to a different sort of growth—a growth in the Lord.

You see, I was an equal opportunity scoffer. That means that my scoffing was not limited to baking or bread. It extended to any number of things that I considered "not necessary for survival." It even extended to how I viewed God's word. Don't get me wrong—I loved God's word. I loved it since it first came alive to me around the age of twelve. And I'd read it. With zeal. In school and college, it just made sense to read it every day. But when I started having babies, those habits and rhythms got squashed. I didn't own my schedule anymore; someone else did. It was my job to keep those "someone elses" alive. Because of this, I wasn't sure how to make my Bible reading fit into every day. It wasn't that there wasn't time; it's that the time was always changing. The routines wouldn't stay put. So some days I'd get to my bed and discover I'd missed my chance.

What made it worse was that I tended to hear two opposite messages from folks I respected about how I should view Bible reading. The first was, "This is only a season. It's okay if you can't get to the Bible every day. God isn't legalistic in his expectations for you. Remember your main responsibility is caring for your kids. Don't be too hard on yourself." Or I heard the opposite message: "There is no excuse for not reading your Bible every day. Set your alarm at 5:00 a.m. if need be! This is God's word, and nothing is more important than that! If you have time to eat, you have time for devotions." Both had validity: God isn't a legalist; I did need to care for my kids; there is nothing more important than knowing God in his word. So I did what many of us are prone to do in our youth—rather than walk forward imperfectly by faith and free of cynicism, I turned that cynicism into a friend who was able to keep me above it all.

I turned to occasionally scoffing—just in my head, mind you. I signed up for a Bible study, then inwardly scoffed at the women who couldn't get their homework done. I also wasn't above scoffing at the woman with more kids than I who seemed to go above and beyond the requirements, bringing nifty pens and highlighters to class and telling us the historical context of our passage. I started a Bible reading plan to read through the Bible in a year, yet I kept side-eyeing others, wondering why some women weren't doing a plan like I was. *Didn't they care about God's word?* This question didn't stop me from also being suspicious toward the motives of the women who always seemed to be nailing the plan with gusto. Just like with the bread, I thought, *Are they just trying to be better than everyone else?*

THE BROAD LAND AND THE GOOD FOOD

Thankfully, my scoffing was increasingly, daily, giving way to desperation for God that kept me glued to the very book that sees through scoffers like me. I was hungry! I needed him more than I needed to be suspicious of others. I needed him to come and inspect my motives more than I needed to inspect others' motives. I needed someone outside of me to speak truth into me—unchanging, unparalleled, saving truth. I needed to see myself and others with the eyes of faith, hope, and love.

So, I'd feed on the scraps at my disposal—a verse I was helping my kids memorize, Scripture songs, my husband's reading of the Bible out loud to us for family devotions. Even these tidbits kept me going on the days I failed to tick the box on the Bible reading plan, which is just like God. Only God's word has *scraps* that can truly satisfy. His word is so nourishing, so powerful, even the nibbles grow us up in him, albeit more slowly than if we were to gulp and devour.

It was only recently that I noticed that my scoffing over those who baked homemade bread and my scoffing over the Bible reading habits of myself and others had coincided. What's more, the scoffing unraveled in proximity. I became a baker of bread about the time I let go of both the guilt-driven, superiority-inducing legalistic way of reading the Bible and the cavalier, licentious way of not reading it. I don't think it's a coincidence. Why? Certainly not because there's anything super spiritual or holy about bread making. No—that's not the case at all. It's because scoffing was the root problem. And scoffing is something that comes from a foolish heart that justifies, whines, and envies.

I needed categories for freedom that I didn't yet have, both in regard to doing simple good works—like baking for my family—and in regard to Bible reading. What if all those bakers *did* know where they could buy bread but chose something different for the sheer satisfaction and enjoyment of it? What if baking for their family was simply a good gift they loved to give? What if the lady who had ticked all the boxes on her "Bible in a year" plan wasn't trying to do better than anyone? What if she was simply more desperate for God? Or more faithful? And what if she was being filled up by him and

therefore happier in him? What if reading my Bible every day—whether consuming small scraps or a feast—wasn't merely my duty, but my delight? What if it was the path to joy on my face, warmth in my heart, and a fat, satisfied soul?

Another wonderful thing began to happen as I kneaded dough and began to understand leaven and experimented with recipes and methods. The passages from the Bible about bread began to be as real and alive to me as the sourdough starter that was growing on my counter. The truth became tangible. It was no accident that Jesus broke an actual loaf of bread when he said, "This is my body, broken for you." It's true that the symbol is just a symbol. It's representative of greater realities, but that doesn't make it unnecessary. The bread is still necessary. Symbols like bread exist to help created people like us begin to understand the one who was not made by human hands.

Elisabeth Elliot said:

The closer one comes to the center of things, the better able he is to observe the connections. Everything created is connected, for everything is produced by the same mind, the same love, and is dependent on the same Creator. He who masterminded the universe, the Lord God Omnipotent, is the One who called the stars into being, commanded light, spoke the Word that brought about the existence of time and space and every form of matter: salt and stone, rose and redwood, feather and fur and fin and flesh.[7]

And, I would add: grains, water, and the great idea of bread in this world. The same God who put it in the hearts of men to make bread with their hands, did so because his Son is the bread not made by human hands, and he makes it his priority to reveal the connections of life to Life, of water to Water, of light to Light, of shepherd to Shepherd, of gate to Gate, of way to Way, of word to Word, and of bread to Bread.

God was showing me just how broad the land is—how utterly spacious and free and happy life is away from scoffing and cynicism. I always knew the gate that leads to life is narrow and that few find it. But I hadn't yet fully realized just where that narrow gate leads. Just where exactly does Jesus take us, when we follow and obey him, when we read and receive every page of the Scriptures as about Jesus, our eternal food?

WISDOM AND FOLLY BOTH OFFER BREAD

Proverbs 9 has two women figures calling out to us, trying to get our attention. One woman is called Wisdom, the other, Folly. Wisdom calls from her well-constructed house:

> *"Whoever is simple, let him turn in here!"*
> *To him who lacks sense she says,*
> *"Come, eat of my bread*
> *and drink of the wine I have mixed.*
> *Leave your simple ways, and live,*
> *and walk in the way of insight." (Prov. 9:4–6)*

Folly likewise calls, but as a loudmouth, a fool, and a seductress:

> *The woman Folly is loud;*
> *she is seductive and knows nothing.*
> *She sits at the door of her house;*
> *she takes a seat on the highest places of the town,*
> *calling to those who pass by,*
> *who are going straight on their way,*
> *"Whoever is simple, let him turn in here!"*
> *And to him who lacks sense she says,*
> *"Stolen water is sweet,*
> *and bread eaten in secret is pleasant."*
> *But he does not know that the dead are there,*
> *that her guests are in the depths of Sheol. (Prov. 9:13–18)*

The question for us is not whether we'll eat bread, but what bread shall we eat? The question isn't whether we'll take a road, but what road will we take? What house will we inhabit? What table will we sit at? What person will we follow?

When we follow Jesus, we are listening to the voice of Wisdom; we are walking in the way of insight. He is taking us to his Father—the one who gives good gifts to his children. Jesus leads us to the vast expanse of eternal life, to freedom, to abundance, to joy in the Father's presence. In that place, we can do good works that aren't proud or ashamed or falsely modest or competing to be seen—we can even do things like make bread or mow the grass or set the table or a million other things with deep enjoyment and love for others. And now that I've had a taste of the freedom, a glimpse of glory, an abundance of *him*, I can't help but beckon you to come as well. The land is good. The food is plenteous. The freedom is not like any other. Won't you come? I'd like to introduce you to the bread of life. I'd like to whet your appetite so that you begin to eat this bread each and every day.

Discussion Questions

1. Are there any areas of life where you are prone to scoffing or cynicism?

2. How can you turn from it?

3. What would it look like to be full of the godly freedom that allows you to act with faith and good will toward the jobs God has given you to do and the people he's put around you?

NO FUSS FOCACCIA

I sometimes think of this recipe as the "four and four twos" recipe.[8] It's how I remember the measurements and ingredients that you'll see below. It's perfect to pair with any Italian food or alongside any main-course meat, or use it as sandwich bread. It's very versatile.

4 cups (544 grams) unbleached all-purpose flour

2 teaspoons (6 or 7 grams) instant yeast

2 teaspoons (8 grams) sugar

2 teaspoons (11 grams) salt

2 cups (474 grams) warm water

Whisk the flour, yeast, sugar, and salt in a large mixing bowl.

Add 2 cups of warm-ish water and mix until a dough is formed and the flour is all absorbed.

Cover and set in a warm spot to rise for at least an hour. (A warm spot can be created by turning your oven on for 1 minute at 350 degrees, then turning it off and putting your dough inside.

Use butter to grease the inside of a 9x13 baking dish.

Gently turn out the dough into the buttered 9x13 dish and drizzle about 2 tablespoons of olive oil onto the dough.

Use fingers to spread out the dough to cover the whole pan.

Sprinkle the surface with salt (sea salt is great) and herbs or veggies of your choice. (I usually do rosemary, basil, or oregano, but in summertime I also add small halved cherry tomatoes. You could also add onions or any herbs you prefer. You can even add eggs on top, which I recommend googling first, but is really fun!).

Let the dough rise while you preheat the oven to 425 degrees.

Bake for 15 minutes at 425 degrees. Reduce the heat to 375 degrees and bake for another 20 minutes.

Let the bread cool and remove from pan.

3

Full Yet Famished

"The LORD is my portion," says my soul,
"therefore I will hope in him."

LAMENTATIONS 3:24

The LORD is my portion;
I promise to keep your words.

PSALM 119:57

G rowing up the youngest of four kids induced in me the unusual ability to hide food. I didn't hide food indiscriminately though, just the good snacks, and actually only one of the good snacks—the peanut butter chocolate chip granola bar. We always had plenty to eat at our house. I didn't know what it was like to be hungry, but I did grow up knowing what it was like to have an inordinate desire for a certain type of granola bar and then miss out on getting one because my older siblings had devoured them before I could nab one. It didn't take me many times of missing out on the longed-for granola bars to start plotting my granola bar acquisition. I would go on high alert when my mom returned from getting groceries. With a very helpful exterior I'd unload all the bags, casually putting things away here and there, while on the inside I was a bird of prey. My eagle eyes could spot the lettering on the granola bar box through the thin, brown, plastic bags.

My mom had a large blue-green glass jar on the counter in our kitchen where any premade snacks were kept. We were allowed to have a snack from the jar only if we got permission. Part of putting away the groceries meant opening any boxes of said snacks, putting them in the jar, and throwing the box away. This made it easy for a young thief like me. I would pocket two of the granola bars and make my way up to my room at my earliest opportunity. I would eat one and stash the other in a large bottom dresser drawer under layers of clothes.

This thieving was, thankfully, short-lived. I recall it happening only a few times. Yet it's the sort of thing I remember even now. Why? Because my conscience knew it was wrong, and I willfully did it anyway—it left an impression on me! If you'd have asked me then what it was exactly that I was doing wrong, I'd probably have put it in the category of disobeying. And that's true—I was disobeying. But a lot more was going on than just disobeying. I was also stealing something actually intended for me because of a sinfully mistrustful and independent spirit.

EVE'S MISPLACED TRUST

When God made Adam and gave him the job of naming all the animals, what became clear was that, as unique and wonderful as each of them were, none would do for Adam. As special as the star-nosed mole, as unparalleled the pink fairy armadillo, and as truly unpredictable the pleasing fungus beetle, there was nary a suitable helper for Adam among the lot. Cue Eve's entrance stage left, or rather right out of Adam's rib. His response did her justice:

> *Then the man said,*
> *"This at last is bone of my bones*
> *and flesh of my flesh;*
> *she shall be called Woman,*
> *because she was taken out of Man." (Gen. 2:23)*

For all the fun a pink fairy armadillo might provide, inspiring Adam's poetic exclamation was not part of its skill set. I imagine Eve was equally glad to behold Adam, although perhaps a bit curious about the entire situation.

We have to assume that Adam got her up to speed, that he was filling her in on God's instructions to him about the trees in the garden—which ones could be eaten from and which *one* couldn't. He was showing her the difference between the ornate horned frog and the Brazilian horned frog. Or perhaps God himself was walking in the garden and telling her all she needed to know. Whatever happened, when the serpent arrived on the scene, she was not ignorant. She expressed herself quite well considering she had just been approached by a talking, crafty creature.

You likely know how the story ends. Despite giving it the old college try, doing her best to restate what she'd been told, Eve succumbed to the temptations of the serpent. She ate the fruit from the tree that they were not to eat from. She disobeyed. Perhaps that's all we're used to seeing when we read that monumental part of the history of mankind. But is there more going on? Sure, she disobeyed, but was that all? Why would she believe a crafty serpent more than the Creator God?

She didn't take from the tree of the knowledge of good and evil because she was being deprived of food. Just like my childhood didn't involve going hungry, neither did Eve's days in the garden. There were plenteous trees for food. Eve's home was the garden. The food in the garden was put there *for her*. She was not fending for herself. So why steal something from your own home? It can only be because the temptation of the serpent had lodged a seed of mistrust toward her Maker. He did so by suggestion, not assertion; by question, not statement. By asking, "Did God actually say?" the serpent subtly invited Eve to stand as judge over God while he simultaneously inserted an exaggeration in his question: "Did God actually say, 'You shall not eat of *any* tree in the garden'?" (Gen. 3:1). Although Eve contradicted the serpent on this point, he had already opened the door for incredulity toward God.

Maybe her Maker wasn't a good provider after all. Maybe he was holding out on her—keeping back the very best and only giving her a sorry second-place provision. Perhaps what she really needed to do in order to be well-provided for was steal from her Father—to start providing for herself.

THE SELF-JUSTIFYING SIN OF ABSTRACTION[9]

The sin that Eve committed lodges in our hearts as well. Whenever we take a rule from our Father and begin examining it apart from him—apart from his character, his fatherly affection, his authoritative goodness—we fall into sin. We become susceptible to lies. Why? Because the rules were never meant to exist apart from the God who gave them to us. Once the serpent had led Eve to begin taking a microscope to God's prohibition,

away from the presence of God and the truth of his character, it isn't any great surprise that his bald-faced lie, "You will not surely die," found hospitality in her newly corrupted mind (Gen. 3:4).

The God from whom life and beauty and provision flow was then seen as a liar and rival. The serpent gave Eve a new way to understand herself and God. This was the first ideology, the first alternative worldview, and, as all ideologies and alternative worldviews have been ever since, it was founded on lies—abstracted from reality. The serpent's system presents "divine love as envy, service as servility, and a suicidal plunge as a leap into life."[10] Eve's eyes departed from her sustainer and Creator and fixed on the rule and the fruit.

Have you ever justified your disobedience to God's words by removing them from the context of his character and authority? What would it sound like to do such a thing? It may sound quite a bit like so much of our "nuanced" excuse-making. We might reason, "Eve was not engaged in any unorthodox behavior. Her confession did not contradict the basic creeds of Christianity. We can see that her interpretation of God's command allowed for her to eat that particular type of fruit. Her conscience was simply formed to allow for her to eat it. Also, we must be generous in understanding that eating fruit is not a sin in and of itself. It certainly doesn't rise to the level of rejecting the deity of Christ or denying the Trinity, after all! This is clearly a tertiary matter about which Christians ought to agree to disagree." I hope that sin-sick reasoning makes you tremble as it does me!

When I tell my son to stay off the grass in our yard, he may initially find that odd or unreasonable. He might be tempted to disobey because when he starts thinking about the grass and looking at it—how nice it looks, how he wants to play soccer on it—he will likely think, "What's wrong with walking on the grass? The grass is perfectly fine!" He doesn't know that the lawn guys just came through and sprayed poison on it to kill the weeds. But if he starts thinking about me, his mom, he's much more likely to obey, because he knows I wouldn't arbitrarily tell him not to walk on the grass. He knows me, so he knows that I must have a good reason, even if it's a reason I haven't shared with him. So, too, with our Father.

How quickly abstraction can turn us all into little sin-justifiers! But none of the instructions and commands and prohibitions of God may be pulled apart from him. We may not doubt *him*—his character and his love—which means we may not doubt the instructions born of that love. We aren't being given arbitrary commands from an automated god. We are being given loving, good commands from a loving, all-powerful, all-knowing, holy God, even when we don't yet fully understand the purposes behind them.

TAKE AND EAT UNTO DEATH, TAKE AND EAT UNTO LIFE

"So when the woman saw that the tree was good for food, and that it was a delight to the eyes, and that the tree was to be desired to make one wise, she took of its fruit and ate, and she also gave some to her husband who was with her, and he ate" (Gen. 3:6). When the first woman "took and ate," she did so unto death. This food would not nourish life—not because the fruit itself was bad, but because eating the fruit was a kind of wicked fruit in and of itself. When God's words of that particular tree, "You shall not eat," had been spit out, vomited up, and discarded by the woman, her heart and mind became hungry for something else, something other than God. Eve, contra the Lord

Jesus, did not make the will of God her food but rejected it so that she could eat the food of sin and death—not the physical fruit alone, but the very words of the tempter in place of God's. Eve ate Satan's words, and the fruit of that was a physical eating that disregarded God and his words.

But when Jesus bids us, "Take and eat," there is no subtle temptation, no great scheme that leads to our demise, but rather Jesus speaks the command as the one who tasted poverty and death on our behalf so that "take and eat become verbs of salvation."[11] He, like his Father, instructs us what to do and is himself the provision. We got it wrong in Eden, the land of delight, separating the instruction from the good instructor, abstracting the command from the command giver, and misunderstanding our provision as merely physical. So Jesus gives us an object lesson from his very flesh and blood—his body is our food. The provider cannot be separated from the provision.

"Take and eat" are costly words. They are a commandment given by the same gracious God who has been providing for us from the beginning.

Perhaps one unanticipated consequence of the theft that happened in the garden is that it cut off Adam and Eve from the joy and spontaneous delight of thankfulness to God. When we are envious and rebellious, when we start acting on our own behalf to get what we have judged ought to be ours, we do not, upon obtaining it, overflow with gratitude. No. Entitled people are not grateful; they are shrivel-souled and grabby.

Oh, but what happiness awaits those who receive God's words as their food and receive his provision for them as from their Father! What untold joy there is in being able to say from the heart, "Thank you, God. I have nothing that I haven't received. Thank you for creating everything. Thank you for life. Thank you for your instructions. Thank you for spiritual provision and physical provision. Thank you even for the trials that have come my way! Thank you, thank you, thank you!" For all things are from him and through him and to him and because we can see that it is so, we get the joy, the happiness, the freedom, of saying thank you.

I never said thank you for those granola bars I pocketed. To do so would have been to admit I'd wrongly taken them. Thankfulness would have been totally inappropriate. What was needed was repentance. Paul gets at this idea when he's reminding us that the grace of God to forgive sin exists so that we would turn from sin, not continue in it (Rom. 6). Similarly, when we discover that our sin of disobedience, theft, and mistrust toward God can be forgiven, we don't keep eating the granola bar and adding, "Thanks, God!" Instead we receive forgiveness and walk in newness of life. We "take and eat" not of the food we've stolen but of the spiritual food freely given by the Son of God—the only one who provides for us food that lasts. Then we let the thankfulness overflow.

Discussion Questions

1. *Can you think of any times when you have separated or abstracted God's words from God himself? How did this impact the way you dealt with his words? How did it change your view of him?*

2. *What are some practical ways you can remind yourself to keep God's words and the loving disposition of God your Father connected as they really are?*

3. *Are there any ways in which you have stolen from God by taking something that he chose to withhold from you? Are you willing to repent and receive the "take and eat" from the mouth of Jesus? If so, give thanks!*

NOT YOUR AVERAGE
ZUCCHINI BREAD

I got this recipe from my mom's good friend Cindy. It has an entire orange in it, peel and all. I'm not going to try to explain why this works—just make it, and you'll see.

3 eggs

1 cup (200 grams) sugar
+ 1 cup (200 grams) sugar

1 cup (240 grams)
vegetable oil

1 teaspoon
(5 grams) vanilla

1 teaspoon (4 grams) salt

2–3 cups (approx 300–350
grams) grated zucchini

1½ teaspoons (7 grams)
baking soda

¼ teaspoon (1 or 2 grams)
baking powder

1½ teaspoons
(3 grams) cinnamon

3 cups (408 grams) flour

1 whole orange
(peel and all)

*makes two loaves

Preheat the oven to 325 degrees.

Cut the unpeeled orange into chunks. Process in a food processor with 1 cup of sugar until smooth.

Combine the orange mix with the rest of the ingredients and mix with a whisk or electric mixer.

Fill greased loaf pans two-thirds full.

Bake for 55 minutes. Test to see if a toothpick comes out clean.

Cool on racks, then remove from the pans.

4

The Wilderness Is for Sight and Sustenance

So she called the name of the Lord who spoke to her, "You are a God of seeing," for she said, "Truly here I have seen him who looks after me."

GENESIS 16:13

The wilderness and the dry land shall be glad;
the desert shall rejoice and blossom like the crocus.

ISAIAH 35:1

This particular wilderness lasted about six years.

I don't know if you've noticed, but seasons in the wilderness tend to have at least two elements: (1) a lack of something we desperately want, and (2) an abundance of something we desperately don't want. The wilderness I was slogging through had a nightmarish lack of sleep and a bumper crop of weekly, if not daily, vomit. I believe I would have eagerly welcomed an actual nightmare had it meant I would have been unconscious, in a real sleep state, for greater than meager minutes and short hours strung together.

Yet the physical manifestations of the wilderness—things like lack of sleep and too much vomit—are never as trying as the deeper realities of what we're being denied and given. I was being denied a healthy, normally sleeping, able-to-eat-by-normal-means, neurotypical son. I was being given a fragile, normally not sleeping, tube-fed son with delays and frightening medical circumstances that made me fear for his life. I longed for certainty about his development. I was being given an abundance of uncertainty and an opportunity to trust God in the midst of it. I intensely wanted to hold my son's life (and our family's life) within my own grasp and take control of the storyline; instead I was held onto by the Lord and propelled into a story I hadn't prepared for. I longed to see our future; I was given a vision of a holy and good God by his word and Spirit.

CATCHING A GLIMPSE OF THE GOD WHO SEES

Hagar found herself in the wilderness not once but twice. The first time, she fled there after Sarai dealt harshly with her. Newly pregnant by Abram and contemptuous of the mistress she was called to submit to, an angel of the Lord came to Hagar. He spoke words of command: "Return to your mistress and submit to her," and words of comfort: "I will surely multiply your offspring so that they cannot be numbered for multitude" (Gen. 16:9–10). In response, Hagar exclaimed a twofold truth—that she had seen the God who sees (Gen. 16:13).

Her second time in the wilderness, God not only saw her but heard the voice of her son and came to do his eye-opening work once again. He opened her eyes so that she could see water, and she and her son were saved. The wilderness exists for sight—both to know that we are seen by God and at last to have our tightly shut eyes opened to see the seeing God.

When we walk through any season of wilderness, the greatest danger is not the scorching heat of the trial or the horrible dryness of the ground; it is that we would be blind to the God who sees us. The greatest danger is that we would begin to believe our wilderness is out of his plan, away from his providing hand, and obscuring his line of sight. We must never believe such deadly things.

It was in the moments of deepest deprivation that I was tempted to question whether God was the seeing God that he has revealed himself to be. Did he see the many nights our bed was soaked—with sheets sopping wet with formula after the tubing disconnected from my son's G-tube in the middle of the night? Had he noticed my new slippers and all my shoes splattered with vomit? Could his eyes penetrate the ceiling of our bedroom, where night after night after night, year after year after year, I tried to comfort my restless, sad, unsettled son, begging him for sleep, begging him for peace? Did he see us in the hospitals, in the PICU, in the ambulances, in the waiting rooms and pre-ops and post-ops? The fact is, he could see, and he did see.

What took me too long to understand was that those circumstances were his gift of sight *to me*. He stripped away so many things I thought I needed, many things I thought I couldn't live without, and in doing so he made one precious and irreplaceable gift come better into focus: himself. He showed himself to be the God of the wilderness. The God who makes streams flow in the desert and who reaps a harvest of fruitfulness in the most unlikely of places.

Our God is the God who sees, and even more than Hagar we have had our eyes opened to see the very image of God, the exact imprint of his nature, the revealing of his glory, very God of very God, our Savior, Redeemer, and perfect friend—the Lord Christ.

TWO WILDERNESSES AND TWO ISRAELS

Not only is the wilderness a place of seeing; it is a place that requires dependence, not self-reliance. This is, of course, where God's covenant people Israel went so terribly wrong.

Israel's wilderness lasted for forty years. It was a result of their disobedience, and it repeatedly showcased their rejection of God. Jesus, who was all that Israel should have been, was in the wilderness for forty days. He was not there as a result of disobedience but because of his obedience to the Spirit, and he repeatedly demonstrated his reliance on God.

When Israel needed physical food or water, God provided it, yet they were not satisfied. Jesus, who could have turned stones to bread, fasted from physical food and water, feasting and being satisfied only by God's words. Israel rejected God's commandments, instead fashioning for themselves a new god to worship in the form of a golden calf and becoming deceivers themselves by saying of idols, "These are your gods, O Israel, who brought you up out of the land of Egypt" (Ex. 32:4). Jesus refused to worship the deceiver, rejecting the glory that comes from the kingdoms of men, and instead spoke the truth: "You shall worship the Lord your God and him only shall you serve" (Matt. 4:10).

Aren't we thankful for the second and better Israel? Doesn't your heart swell to see him do what the first Israel couldn't? Aren't you encouraged that your wilderness season is

overseen and orchestrated by the God who provides a way to escape temptation? Unlike Eve, who took physical food offered her by the tempter in order to try to gain power and divinity, Jesus refused physical food offered by the tempter *as a sign of his power and divinity*. Unlike the Israelites who were unhappy with the daily provision of God, Jesus is satisfied by the provision of God's every word. Jesus saw beyond the wilderness and the cross to the joy set before him at God's right hand so that we can look to Jesus in the midst of our own wilderness (Heb. 12:2).

THE BREAD OF ADVERSITY THAT LEADS TO SIGHT

Isaiah prophesied, "Though the Lord give you the bread of adversity and the water of affliction, yet your Teacher will not hide himself anymore, but your eyes shall see your Teacher. And your ears shall hear a word behind you, saying, 'This is the way, walk in it,' when you turn to the right or when you turn to the left" (Isa. 30:20).

We have a teacher whom our eyes have seen and our ears have heard. He is leading us by his word. Whether you are in a dark night of the soul or experiencing chronic pain or disease or persecution from the authorities or a very hard marriage or unwanted divorce or miscarriage or cancel culture or disability or joblessness, his word is saying to you, "This is the way, walk in it." The wilderness is a surprisingly *safe place* for us, sisters, the safest place of all. Don't get me wrong—the wilderness doesn't ensure the earthly outcomes we want, but it does ensure our dependence on him. Danger lies all around in worldly comfort, earthly riches, status, fame, and independence, but the wilderness is free of those traps. It gives us one thing we desperately don't want: the bread of adversity; but it also gives us an abundance of something we desperately need: eyes to see our teacher and ears to hear his word and receive it as our food—"This is the way, walk in it."

Discussion Questions

1. *Have you been or are you currently in a wilderness season? What things are you being denied? What are you being given?*

2. *What is the greatest spiritual danger for you in this wilderness? What is the greatest spiritual provision?*

3. *How can you lean on and trust the God who sees you? How can you share with others what you've seen of the Lord and the deep lessons he's taught you in the wilderness?*

WEEKNIGHT NAAN

This is a regular at our house all year round.[12] It's just plain good. Our favorite dishes to eat it with are Butter Curry Chicken and Street Cart Chicken.

½ cup (118 grams) warm water

1 teaspoon (4 grams) sugar

2¼ teaspoons (7 grams) instant yeast

2½ cups (340 grams) all-purpose flour (you may want slightly less or slightly more flour—the stickier your dough, the more delicate and chewy the naan will be, but the more difficult to roll out)

½ cup (123 grams) yogurt (Greek honey or vanilla flavored work well)

½ teaspoon (2 grams) salt

1 tablespoon (14 grams) oil

vegetable oil, for greasing the skillet

3 tablespoons (60 grams) melted butter (optional)

makes 8 pieces

Combine the warm water, sugar, and yeast in a medium/large mixing bowl. Whisk together.

Add the flour, yogurt, salt, and oil. Mix with a large spoon until roughly combined.

Turn out on a floured counter and knead by hand for about 10 minutes until the dough is smooth. You may need to add small amounts of flour if the dough is too sticky.

Place the dough in a clean bowl, cover it, and let it rise for about 1 hour (until it is doubled in size).

Turn the dough out on the counter and divide it into 8 equal parts using a bench scraper or knife.

Roll out each piece into a circle or oblong shape (approx. 8 inches in diameter) using a rolling pin.

Pour vegetable oil in a skillet (cast iron or nonstick—whatever you've got will work) and set the stove to medium-high heat.

In the pan fry each piece of rolled-out dough, turning each piece over when it starts to puff up and bubble. Continue cooking, adding more oil to the pan when necessary.

Brush with melted butter and serve.

5

When the Manna Isn't Quite What We Were Expecting

As the living Father sent me, and I live because of the Father,
so whoever feeds on me, he also will live because of me.

JOHN 6:57

"What is it?"

The answer is so simple: it was God's miraculous heavenly provision for his people. It was manna. It was how God would keep them from starving (Ex. 15, 31).

But there was a little more to it. Manna was also how God would humble an exasperated and frustrated people. Manna was a lot like a stone of offense. God gave his people food, and they offered up more complaining than toddlers on a ten-hour road trip.

A SACRIFICE OF GRUMBLING

We had funnel cakes for Good Friday. That may not be the most obvious choice for what is arguably the holiest and most somber day of the Christian calendar, but at the time, our kids were two, four, six, and eight. Plus we had a five-month-old taking up residence in my womb. Our house was for sale, which meant every day I devoted myself to make-believe—make-believe that four small children didn't live here. Make-believe that we were modern and minimalistic. Make-believe that we were the kind of people whose hangers all match. Make-believe that we produced only pleasant smells. Make-believe that we had no need to cook or do laundry. And the most fantastical of all: make-believe that I was an interior designer.

Yet our spirits were high on this particular Good Friday, and funnel cakes just seemed like the thing to do. It was time to throw caution aside and embrace our inner state-fair aficionado. It was time to risk oil splats and batter spills and choking on powdered sugar inhaled to the inner crevices of the lungs. It was time to risk the shame of enjoying a food so utterly bereft of all the things that make for respectable food nowadays.

I couldn't help but think of manna. Manna, after all, was "like coriander seed, white, and the taste of it was like wafers made with honey" (Ex. 16:31)—a grain that actually fell from heaven. When God's people first saw it, it looked like frost covering the ground. It seems that bread from heaven would be cause for great rejoicing, but if that happened,

we don't hear about it. And as much as we enjoyed the funnel cakes that day, it wasn't too hard for me to imagine how unpleasant such sweetness would become if it were our sole sustenance for *forty years*. I've always been a savory sort of gal, so sweet without salty on repeat gives me a sickly feeling.

The Israelites and I have quite a bit in common, it turns out. They weren't impressed by the manna despite its miraculous nature, at least not after having consumed it for days on end. So rather than offer God a sacrifice of praise for his provision, at least some of them joined together in a fussy ruckus:

> *Now the rabble that was among them had a strong craving. And the people of Israel also wept again and said, "Oh that we had meat to eat! We remember the fish we ate in Egypt that cost nothing, the cucumbers, the melons, the leeks, the onions, and the garlic. But now our strength is dried up, and there is nothing at all but this manna to look at. (Num. 11:4–6)*

There was a diet that health-conscious folks could get behind: fish, cucumbers, melons, leeks, onions, and garlic. Hello, paleo. I mean, why wouldn't God want them to eat something with so many nutritional benefits? Why would the Creator of the world and everything in it—including every type of fruit, vegetable, and meat—display his power to sustain them with a single flaky sweet grain?

My answer is likely not a complete one, but I think the Lord may have chosen a single grain at least partially because he didn't want them to depend on the food in and of itself, but on him. We must not be so taken by the provision that we forget the provider. Yet there they were, begging to return to Egypt, completely deluded about what life was like there. Their memories were failing them. They remembered food that "cost nothing." Nothing—except for that small matter of it costing them their very lives. They were slaves in Egypt. The food wasn't free. They weren't free. Their children weren't free. Yet how quickly this unwanted manna had rewritten the past for them.

The Israelites grumbled so much that God finally gave them some meat to eat. At last, some protein. But it didn't work out quite how they'd hoped:

Therefore the LORD will give you meat, and you shall eat. You shall not eat just one day, or two days, or five days, or ten days, or twenty days, but a whole month, until it comes out at your nostrils and becomes loathsome to you, because you have rejected the LORD who is among you and have wept before him, saying, "Why did we come out of Egypt?" (Num. 11:18–20)

The Israelites wept before God. They cried and begged in the midst of what was undoubtedly a traumatic experience, yet it seems not all tears are virtuous, even if they're sincere. Does that shock you, bother you, make you question God's goodness? Am I allowed to say that our tears, *my tears*, need to be objectively evaluated to discover whether they are sinful? Have you ever indulged in watching your own tears drip down your face as you took stock of how truly pitiful you were? I have. If you want to know if your crying is selfish drivel that God frowns at, this might be a helpful test: *Am I tempted to watch the tears stream down in the mirror?* Am I trying to impress God or others with my misery—certain that the realness of my feelings will obligate him to do what I want?

The mirror tends to make gods of us all, whether we come to it with legit crying or self-manipulation. If we think that feeling sorry for ourselves has anything to do with the robust complaints and laments offered to God in the psalms, it's time to stop staring in the mirror. Yes, cry out to God, but do so by faith and with trust that he knows best, even as he stores those tears in his bottle (Ps. 56:8).

VALIDATION COMING OUT OUR NOSES

When we weep to ourselves with delusional self-pity and ungrateful grumbling against the God who rescued us from slavery and provides for our every need, God does not smile. But he does act. The Lord gave the grumblers exactly what they asked for. He gave them even more than they asked for—more than they imagined.

But this was not a wish fulfillment given by a genie in a bottle at the ready to do what he's told. This was the wise discipline of the great I Am—the one who multiplied gnats and frogs and hail and boils and blood in the Nile in order to rescue these very people. Had they forgotten that he would have no trouble multiplying meat until they choked on it? But their hearts had hardened just like Pharaoh's, and it would take some more hard-hitting signs and wonders to recapture their attention and respect.

When we weep in foolish distrust of God that grows into self-absorbed pity, I think God often gives us exactly what we ask for—he validates our plight with sickening amounts of figurative meat. For us, the validation comes from both our own inner dialogue and from the folks around us who feel badly for us. But aren't we supposed to "weep with those who weep"? you may ask. Yes and amen. But remember that the sentence just prior commands, "Rejoice with those who rejoice" (Rom. 12:15). Yet we instinctively know we shouldn't rejoice with another's joy over wrongdoing and sin. That makes nonsense of the Bible.

Likewise, not all tears are wet with virtue. Not all weeping should be shored up with solidarity. Beware of the treachery that can hide in our own sobs. You might discover God will give you the validation you so desperately desire until it's coming out of your nose. If he does, now is as good a time as any to turn from self-validation and the validation of others and to seek the approval of God. God has done right by us. He has taken pity on us. Is it enough that he takes thought for you (Ps. 40:17)? We must not dishonor him by acting as though it's our job to take thought for ourselves.

OKAY, BUT WHAT IS *THIS*?

When Jesus shows up on the scene in the Gospel of Mark, he keeps astonishing everyone. Mark didn't get the memo about not reusing the same words in your writing. He keeps saying "amazed" and "astonished" and, my favorite, "*immediately.*" But, since God is the real author of Mark's Gospel, we know that the repetition is not for lack of a thesaurus. It is not due to limited vocabulary. The repetition is there to help us. Jesus amazes and astonishes everyone with signs and wonders as he delivers them from sickness, disease, sin, and bondage, just like Yahweh amazed and astonished everyone with signs and wonders when he delivered his people from bondage and slavery.

After Jesus's first show of miraculous power in the Gospel of Mark (his healing of a man with an unclean spirit), the amazed people turn to each other and say, "What is this?" (Mark 1:27). In the Septuagint, which is a Greek version of the Old Testament

that Jesus and the Jewish people of the day used, that phrase, "What is this?" is the exact same phrase that the Israelites uttered when they first saw the manna in the wilderness and turned to each other saying, "What is it?"[13] The same Greek phrase is translated as "What is it?" and "What is this?" This echo of the exodus story, this repetition of phrase, is an early tip-off of what the apostle John makes explicit. Jesus is the bread come down from heaven. He is our miraculous heavenly provision.

The people seek a sign from Jesus as explicit as the manna their forefathers ate, asking him, "Then what sign do you do, that we may see and believe you? What work do you perform? Our fathers ate the manna in the wilderness; as it is written, 'He gave them bread from heaven to eat'" (John 6:30–31). They seek a sign like bread falling from heaven not because it would make them believe, but because *they were bent on not believing.* They seek a sign of raining grain, even though they had watched him multiply bread for a multitude. They are disingenuous. They don't care about signs. They want to be in control of the situation. So Jesus answers them:

> *Truly, truly, I say to you, whoever believes has eternal life. I am the bread of life. Your fathers ate the manna in the wilderness, and they died. This is the bread that comes down from heaven, so that one may eat of it and not die. I am the living bread that came down from heaven. If anyone eats of this bread, he will live forever. And the bread that I will give for the life of the world is my flesh.* (John 6:47–51)

What is this? This is the bread of heaven standing in your midst. If you refuse to eat it—which means to believe in him—there can be no eternal life, but only an expectation of death.

THE BREAD OF OFFENSE

I remember my face getting hot as though someone had turned on a stove inside my body. I read my email with distress. The words from this dear fellow Christian were rebuking me in a way that seemed to sink right into the deepest parts of me—I felt uncomfortably seen and hurt. My mind quickly began to work my way out of it—looking for the errors in the email, the sentences that could have been more accurate, the ways I hadn't been understood properly, which were real enough.

Yet, I could see opposing paths before me—the path of self-justification or the path of repentance, the path of offended-ness or the path of humility, the path of life or the path of death. I could rebuff this rebuke as hurtful and demeaning, or I could receive it as the faithful wounds of a friend, sent to me for my welfare by the God who is working all things for my good. All I knew of this person—a faithful life, a humble demeanor, a teachable spirit, wisdom and knowledge of the word—was begging me to take this rebuke seriously. And with the help of God's Spirit at work in me, I did take it seriously. It remains with me to this day as oil on my head and nourishment for my bones.

When Jesus's many disciples heard his narrow and seemingly outrageous statements that not only was he the manna come down from heaven, the bread of life, but that they must eat of his flesh in order to have eternal life, they had two paths before them. They could grumble and be offended and leave, or they could turn to him as the way, the truth, and the life—the true bread from heaven. And both of those things happened. Some grumbled as Jesus asked them, "Do you take offense at this?" (John 6:61). We know they did take offense, because many of his disciples "turned back and no longer walked with him" after his teaching (John 6:66). But not all. Some remained. "So Jesus said to the twelve, 'Do you want to go away as well?' Simon Peter answered him, 'Lord, to whom shall we go? You have the words of eternal life, and we have believed, and have come to know, that you are the Holy One of God'" (John 6:67–69).

The bread of Jesus is the bread of offense. There is no way around it. If you follow him, if you receive him, if you love him, if you die his death and live his life, then you too will be offensive. Like my friend who was willing to rebuke and offend me for my good, you will be offensive to many because you don't live to please them or to be liked by them, but you live for the Lord and by every word that comes from his mouth. Because of that, a counterintuitive thing happens: we can actually love our friends and neighbors with the offense of Christ, knowing that for some it will not be mere offense or a stone of stumbling, but true life—the precious cornerstone on which they stand.

The manna isn't quite what we were expecting—it is eternally better—it is Jesus Christ.

Discussion Questions

1. *How do you respond when you don't get what you want? What do you think might happen if God did give you everything you want?*

2. *Are you offended by Jesus's claim to be the true bread from heaven that gives life?*

3. *Which is better: the thing you think you want or the gift of offensive bread that leads to eternal life? What would it look like for you to stop trying to control what gifts God offers you and instead receive Jesus for who he is?*

CHEESE BREAD

This cheese bread is a wonderful combination of a crunchy crust and a soft inside.[14] It is also cheesy, which means that no matter what happens, it will be good. You can sprinkle on some oregano and basil and dip it in marinara sauce for a fun pizza vibe.

6¼ cups (794 grams) unbleached all-purpose or bread flour

2 teaspoons (14 grams) salt

5 tablespoons (64 grams) brown sugar or granulated sugar

1 cup (237 grams) warm water

1 cup plus a splash more (250 grams) warm milk or buttermilk

1½ teaspoons (14 grams) instant yeast

¼ cup (57 grams) melted butter or vegetable oil

2½ cups (340 grams) shredded cheese (I like mozzarella and parmesan, but any hard cheese works)

makes two loaves

Whisk the flour, salt, and sugar in a large bowl.

Combine the water and buttermilk and yeast in a separate bowl. Whisk together.

Pour the wet ingredients into the dry ingredients. Add the melted butter. Mix it all together with a large spoon or dough hook until combined or for a few minutes.

Leave the dough to rest for 5 to 10 minutes.

Mix the dough for another 3 or so minutes until it is soft and tacky but not sticky (you can add flour if needed).

Turn the dough out onto a floured counter and knead for 1 to 2 minutes. Shape it into a ball.

Place the dough in clean bowl (it helps to spray the bowl with cooking spray so that the dough doesn't get stuck to the bowl) and let it rise at room temperature for 60–90 minutes, or until it doubles in size. (If you prefer, you can put the dough in the refrigerator overnight or up to three days, then, on the day you want to bake, remove from the fridge and let it come to room temperature. Proceed with the instructions).

Turn the dough out onto a floured counter and divide it into two pieces.

continued on page 81

Dust the dough with flour and roll it out to rectangles approximately 8 inches wide and 12 inches long.

Divide the cheese evenly and spread half on each rolled-out rectangle.

Roll up the rectangles lengthwise into logs and use fingertips to seal the edge.

Place loaves either on a parchment-lined cookie sheet or in loaf pans.

Cover the loaves with a tea towel and let them rise for approximately 90 minutes on the counter.

15 minutes before baking, preheat the oven to 350 degrees.

Bake at 350 for 20 minutes. Rotate the pans and bake for 30 more minutes. (The bread should have a deep golden color and an internal temperature of at least 185 degrees.)

Cool on a cooling rack for 30 minutes (or until no longer hot), slice, and serve.

6

A Little Leaven for Good or Ill

He told them another parable. "The kingdom of heaven is like leaven that a woman took and hid in three measures of flour, till it was all leavened."

MATTHEW 13:33

Jesus said to them, "Watch and beware of the leaven of the Pharisees and Sadducees."

MATTHEW 16:6

About four years ago I started a little science experiment on my counter that's as old as time. It's called "sourdough starter." All you do is mix equal parts flour and water and wait. After a couple of days, add some more flour and water. A day or so later, dump some out and add some more flour and water. Repeat every day to old age and gray hairs.

That flour-and-water concoction on my counter is what used to be called "leaven." It's a bit of dough that has fermented. That leaven, when added to a large lump of dough, makes it rise and turns it into bread. What looks utterly unremarkable to the eye—indistinguishable from regular dough—is actually alive and growing, as long as it's being fed.

There are two important characteristics of leaven, both actual leaven and spiritual leaven. (1) Leaven is hidden. You can't see it once it's mixed into the dough. Similarly, spiritual leaven works in secret, in the heart, mind, and soul. (2) Leaven is a change agent. It doesn't leave dough the way it was. It works its way through it and turns it into something else. Spiritual leaven changes people and groups of people—it doesn't leave them as they are—whether for good or ill.

I had the honor of attending a funeral recently for a ninety-nine-year-old man of God named Gordy. I'd only met him once or twice and didn't know him much at all. His children, grandchildren, and great-grandchildren all honored him over the course of the service with stories, songs, and reflections on the constancy and faithfulness of his life—a life poured out for God and for others, stable and sturdy because it was fastened to God's word.

As I listened, watched, and read about him, everything seemed familiar. It was like I was smelling an aroma of bread that I'd smelled before; I was tasting a sweetness that had been on my tongue before; I could recognize this man as easily as if I was his grandchild. How is that possible, considering I didn't know him personally? It's possible because the leaven of his godly life had worked its way through the life of his grandson, Jon, whom I know very well and who is a pastor of my church. Ninety-nine-year-old Gordy could

be tasted in his grandson, my brother in Christ. And that good leaven had spread not only to Jon but also to Jon's wife and children and, in some measure, even to our family.

NO GENERIC LEAVEN

Leaven is particular to its geographical area. Every sourdough starter draws bacteria from the air and has a peculiarity—a certain taste and flavor profile. So, while all leaven is the same thing (flour and water) and does the same thing (acts as yeast working through dough), each sourdough starter is also slightly distinctive. The best example is San Francisco sourdough. You can't make San Francisco sourdough anywhere other than in the city of San Francisco. Why? Because the flavor profile of the bacteria in San Francisco's air is distinctive. Some say it's because of the large amount of a particular strain of bacteria in the air that isn't as present in other parts of the country and world. Others give credit to the frequent fog, which provides a bacteria-rich environment for yeast to live in the air. In any case, San Francisco's sourdough is unique and has become internationally acclaimed.

It's like Gordy's life. All Christians are like leaven in the world, and all are composed of the same thing—Jesus's perfect life, his death on the cross, and his resurrection to eternal life. We all do essentially the same thing: we walk in a manner worthy of the gospel by loving others, believing and proclaiming the truth of God's word, and growing up into Christ. Yet each of us is unique, and the leaven of our lives has a distinct flavor profile. Gordy was a man of humble service. That came through in the leaven of his life passed to his family and friends.

Have you pondered what sort of leaven your life might be passing on? What flavor is being picked up by those nearest to you? What will you have spread to those around you when it's time to tell stories at your funeral?

MULTIPLYING THE LEAVEN OF MEEKNESS

Many years ago when we had only three very small children, the Lord put a longing for meekness in my heart. I'm reasonably bold, and I'm usually a direct communicator, so "meek" (at least the stereotype of it) seems miles away from my natural inclinations. But I'd seen in myself inward disturbances—sort of like a boiling pot of water. I was increasingly stirred up about things, a little frothy and unsettled. Anything from parenting challenges, to the news, to politics, to small (or big) relational tensions, to a heretical book or a wayward public Christian figure could get my insides roiling. I longed to be the sort of person who is unflappable and whose inner spirit is peaceful no matter the outer circumstances.

Soon after this desire for meekness was awakened in me, I attended a Christian conference and was perusing the speaker-recommended books when I came across one with a title I couldn't ignore: *The Quest for Meekness and Quietness of Spirit* by Matthew Henry.[15] *Eureka!* That was precisely the quest I was on. Since that time, I've read the book more times than I can count. I've meditated on the parts in Scripture where meekness is highlighted. My quest (and subsequent growing acquisition, by God's grace) for meekness has been a powerful agent for change in my inner life, and it's one I'd like to pass along, a little bit like I were sharing my sourdough starter with you.

Matthew Henry tells about a man who would say on his way to hear the word, "Now let the word of the Lord come; and if I had six hundred necks, I would bow them all to the authority of it."[16] James tells us to receive the implanted word with meekness (James 1:21); surely this man's attitude is what he has in mind. Henry says:

> To receive the word with meekness is to be delivered into it [the word] as a mold. ... Meekness softens the wax, that it may receive the impression of the seal, whether it be "for doctrine or reproof, for correction or instruction in righteousness." It opens the ear to discipline, silences objections, and suppresses the risings of the carnal mind against the word.[17]

Not only is meekness the posture in which we receive, with a hand over our often loud and objecting mouths, the word as our authority. It is also "the silent submission of the soul to the providence of God concerning us."[18] This! This was the answer to my quest! Meekness would not curb reasonable boldness or my propensity for direct speech—that wasn't its aim—but it would teach my heart to be silent and soft before the word and the providence of our perfect God. It would train my emotions to kneel before him, much to their eternal joy. It would be the effectual words "Peace, be still" spoken to my inner waves of turmoil. Meekness is the bit in the mouth of the horse, the rudder guiding the whole ship, the inner peace that passes understanding because of a deep and abiding trust in the Lord.

You might wonder why I'm inserting meekness into this conversation about leaven. It's simply because I believe meekness is about as close to the heart of Jesus as we can get. It is invisible, yet powerful, and it is the sort of leaven I want to spread as far and wide as possible. It's also because meekness is scorned in this world far beyond other virtues. It is frequently trampled by believer and unbeliever alike. Women take offense at it, terrified that they are being singled out in Peter's epistle when he admonishes them: "Let your adorning be the hidden person of the heart with the imperishable beauty of a gentle [meek] and quiet spirit, which in God's sight is very precious" (1 Pet. 3:4). And let's not pretend otherwise—*we are being singled out!* What a blessing! We are blessed by the Lord when he tells us to throw off the horribly impossible yoke of trying to achieve or maintain outward beauty and take up the cause for inward beauty—meekness—which is precious to God and lasts forever.

BEWARE THE HIDDEN LEAVEN OF HYPOCRISY

The Scriptures refer to leaven as a good thing only a handful of times in association with the spreading of the kingdom of God. But well over a dozen times, it warns about leaven as a symbol of sin. This ought to make us quite leery of how easily sin spreads. It's gangrenous. It doesn't just spread; it sours and infects.

More pointedly, sinful leaven is composed of a particular strain of bacteria that tends to dominate the flavor profile of hidden sin. It's called hypocrisy. Jesus warns his disciples to, "Beware of the leaven of the Pharisees, which is hypocrisy. Nothing is covered up that will not be revealed, or hidden that will not be known" (Luke 12:1–2). In calling out the particular source of bad leaven as hypocrisy, Jesus is giving us a tip-off about how inward sin corrupts the soul, making even extremely scrupulous and religious people into children of the devil (John 8:44).

One of the hands-down most important things Christian parents or Christian mentors teach their kids or mentees is how *not* to be a hypocrite—which is another way of saying, we teach them to be the same person everywhere they go, even (maybe especially) in private, when no one but God is watching. Even when they aren't living up to what we desire for them in terms of godliness, it's very important that nobody fake it.

Growth in the Lord may be slow; sinful patterns may persist, but those things can, with God's grace in Christ and the power of his Spirit, be chipped away and sanctified over time. What is exceedingly difficult to fix is an entrenched hypocrite—someone who has become duplicitous, who acts on pretense. The reason a hypocrite is so very hard to guide and direct toward less hypocrisy and more integrity is twofold. First, the nature of hypocrisy is hidden. Often the people around hypocrites aren't aware of their hypocrisy and may be falling for the pretense. Second, and even worse, hypocrites are usually self-deceived. They begin to believe their own pretense and have lost touch with reality, just like the Pharisees, who had so twisted God's word that they didn't know its main point but only their additions to it.

If we think on our own past, it's likely each of us can think of some hypocritical thing we have done or may currently be doing. Most of the hypocrisy in my life has been evidenced when I've expected things of my kids that I'm not practicing. I want them to be quick to listen, slow to speak, and slow to become angry, but I've been quick to interrupt, slow to listen, and hasty in my irritation. When we notice the distance between our behavior and our beliefs, sometimes we think *that* is the hypocrisy, but it isn't—or at least it may not be. The hypocrisy is the pretense, the lie, that we are better or different than we are. Our lives will never live up to or perfectly match our beliefs; only Jesus can do that. The Lord reminds us through John that if we say we have no sin, we deceive ourselves and the truth is not in us (1 John 1:8). Hypocrisy isn't a person who says sinning is wrong yet still sins, but a person who pretends she doesn't sin when of course she does, and in so doing, compounds sin with sin.

And that's just what the Pharisees did. Not only did they disregard and make a mockery of God's actual law by ignoring the weighty matters and making up their own traditions in its place; they also did all that while loading down others with heavy burdens that they themselves would not lift. They were two-faced.

HYPOCRISY HIDES IN TRIBES

If you've spent five seconds on Twitter or anywhere on social media, you know that our entire globe has divided into little (and big) tribes. These tribes are self-congratulatory echo chambers. They pat each other on the back for thinking all the same things and condemn and deride other tribes for not thinking those same things. They have lost any whiff of intellectual honesty and strictly protect themselves from self-examination. These communities help us understand why and how hypocrisy is frequently a group endeavor.

Individuals are all responsible for their own hypocrisy, but hypocrisy thrives in the dim light of tribalism. It needs "friends" to keep repeating the lies as though they were truth. It finds comfort in the presence of others who affirm its false view of reality. This was the particular problem of the Pharisees—they were an entire group of hypocrites because they affirmed each other's false ideas. This sort of group blindness can happen to anyone.

The Corinthians had to decide whether to call out sin or pretend that bad leaven didn't exist among them. Paul writes to them, rightly outraged, that in their church, a man had his father's wife. But what really piqued Paul was their *arrogance* in the midst of the sexual sin! It's one thing to sin sexually; it's another to be proud about it, acting like everything's great. That's the sort of leaven that hypocrisy leads to—bold-faced

pride and arrogance and an inability to see sin for what it is. The Lord says through Paul to the Corinthians:

> Your boasting is not good. Do you not know that a little leaven leavens the whole lump? Cleanse out the old leaven that you may be a new lump, as you really are unleavened. For Christ, our Passover lamb, has been sacrificed. Let us therefore celebrate the festival, not with the old leaven, the leaven of malice and evil, but with the unleavened bread of sincerity and truth. (1 Cor. 5:6–8)

The cure for the Corinthians' bad leaven of arrogance, boasting, malice, and evil was Christ, the Passover Lamb. When God freed the Israelites from slavery in Egypt, he did so with signs and wonders that culminated in sending the angel of death to kill every firstborn child. The Israelites were spared from that fate by sacrificing a lamb. "Then they shall take some of the blood and put it on the two doorposts and the lintel of the houses in which they eat it. They shall eat the flesh that night, roasted on the fire; with unleavened bread and bitter herbs they shall eat it" (Ex. 12:7–8).

Because of Christ our Passover Lamb, who was sacrificed as an atonement for our sins, we are able to "cleanse out the old leaven" as Paul instructs. The Israelites were commanded, as they waited for the angel of death to pass over them, to eat only unleavened bread to symbolize their purity and holiness. The new-covenant command is that *we ourselves* are to be unleavened because we are part of an unleavened people—a people set apart for holiness, not a people who make a hiding place for group hypocrisy. We don't just avoid leaven in our bread for one week as in the old covenant, but we are unleavened people every day, always. When God's people, the church, gather together, it is to celebrate our Passover Lamb as we feast on the unleavened bread of sincerity and truth. That's what unites us. That's what makes the people of God different from hypocritical tribalism—our hearts have been purified by the blood of Christ, and we are free to turn from our sins and repent of hypocrisy with restored and sincere hearts. This, dear readers, is magnificent news.

HIDDEN ONLY FOR A TIME

Leaven is hidden until it isn't. Eventually it becomes unmistakable. It is revealed as either the leaven of the kingdom of heaven bearing the fruit of meekness and love and humility or the leaven of hypocrisy bearing the stench of pretense, lying, and hate. Ultimately, what's revealed is who gave us that leaven to begin with: did it come from our heavenly Father, with a heavenly purpose, or is it from the father of lies—a putrid, spoiled wreck? We don't have to wait until that final judgment day to ask God to search us and inspect our hearts and see if there is any unclean way in us. We can do that now.

And what's more, because we know God is a good God, who provides for us in every way, especially spiritually, we can rest secure knowing that by his Spirit he will actually do it. He loves us. He has made a way to cleanse out the old leaven and has supplied the new heart of sincerity and truth that we so desperately need.

Discussion Questions

1. Can you discern any strains of hypocritical leaven in your life? Have you protected yourself from seeing this hypocrisy with tribalism?

2. What are some steps you can take to clean out the bad leaven and become what you really are in Christ?

3. Is there any particular godly strain of Christlike leaven that you would like to spread to those around you? What is it? Ask God to help you do it.

SOURDOUGH STARTER & SOURDOUGH COUNTRY LOAF

If you've ever wanted to try your hand at sourdough, here's your chance to start your own "starter" and make sourdough bread.[19] Patience is required, but it's worth it. You'll notice the recipe uses only grams for measurements, so if you want to do this, you'll need a kitchen scale. If you read through this recipe and find you need video help, I've made some tutorials that you can find online.[20]

START YOUR OWN STARTER

*It takes 5–7 days for your starter to be ready to make bread.

Mix 100 grams of flour (unbleached all-purpose flour works fine) with 100 grams of water in a bowl or jar.

Cover with a tea towel and let it sit on a counter for 2–3 days. Bubbles should begin to form on the top.

After two or three days, begin discarding at least half of the starter each day and refreshing it with 50 grams of flour and 50 grams of water.

After about one week, you should notice that the starter rises several hours after being fed, then falls in between feedings. This means it is ready to use to make bread.

The night before making bread, discard all but 1–2 tablespoons of the starter. Add 200 grams of flour and 200 grams of water. This is called "leaven." When you use it to make bread, you will have some left over, which is your starter that you keep feeding each day.

200 grams (¾ cup) leaven

700 grams (5⅝ cups) warm water

850 grams (6¾ cups) unbleached all-purpose flour

150 grams (1 cup) wheat flour

30 grams (1½ tablespoons) salt

makes two loaves

TWO DAYS BEFORE BAKING:

Refresh your starter so that you will have leaven the next day. (See "Start Your Own Starter" for how to turn your starter into leaven.)

THE DAY BEFORE BAKING:

Pour the warm water into a large mixing bowl. Add the leaven to the water (it should float if it's healthy and ready to use). Dissolve the leaven into the water with your hands.

Add the unbleached all-purpose flour, wheat flour, and salt.

Using your hands or a large spoon or a dough hook, mix the ingredients together until a shaggy mass is formed and no dry flour remains.

Let the dough rest for 20 minutes.

Mix the dough again for about 1 to 2 minutes, then cover with a tea towel and let it rise for 30 minutes in a warm environment (you can create this environment by turning your oven on at 350 degrees for 1 minute, then turning it off and placing the dough inside the oven).

With wet hands, stretch and fold the dough by lifting up the underneath edge of the dough, pulling it up to stretch it, then folding it on top of itself. Do this four times, rotating the bowl so you get each side of the dough.

Repeat the stretch-and-fold technique three more times, letting the dough rise 1 hour in between stretch and folds.

Turn the dough out on a floured counter and divide it into two pieces with a bench scraper.

Fold the dough from the outsides into the middle, then place each piece seam side down on the counter, with the taut side up. Cover with a towel and let it rest for 20 minutes.

continued on following pages

Turn both pieces of dough back over with the seam side up (the dough will have lost some of its shape). Reshape the dough by pulling out the four corners of the dough to make it flat, then taking two corners and folding them onto the center, then folding the other two corners on top of those. Roll the dough over so that the seams are down again and the taut side is on top. Do the same to the other piece of dough.

Place the loaves seam side up, taut side down, into lined, floured shaping baskets (or bowls lined with a floured tea towel). Cover with plastic wrap.

Put the covered dough in the refrigerator overnight (or up to three days).

ON BAKING DAY:

Take the dough out of the fridge and let it sit on the counter while the oven preheats.

Preheat the oven to 500 degrees with the Dutch oven or cast iron pot inside (with lids on).

Once the oven and pots are preheated, cut two pieces of parchment paper and lightly flour them.

Flip the dough out onto the parchment paper (now the seam will be down again and the taut side up). Score the top of the dough with a sharp knife or razor blade (this allows the dough to expand while baking).

Pick up the parchment paper with the dough on it and put it in the Dutch oven or cast iron pot. Put lids on the pots.

Bake at 500 degrees for 20 minutes.

Reduce the heat to 450 degrees and remove the lids. Bake for 20–25 more minutes or until the bread is a golden or deep brown.

Remove and let the bread cool on cooling racks for 30 minutes or until cool.

7

Better a Crumb from the Right Table than a Feast at the Wrong One

She said, "Yes, Lord, yet even the dogs eat the crumbs that fall from their masters' table."

MATTHEW 15:27

I remember the conversation very clearly. I had recently been told by our son's neurologist that it was a very real possibility that he wouldn't live past his second birthday. I was in the throes of something like grief, but not quite. It was more like the look of someone whose car is spinning on black ice on the freeway, with terror in her eyes. I can't say that much of what I was doing was premeditated or intentional during those days. I was just desperately loving my son and trying to keep my heart from crumbling out of my chest into a pile on the floor. God was holding us all together. I remember times of laughter and an almost exquisite pain in the center of the joy. Such are trials.

It was during that white-knuckling time that this memorable conversation took place. A fellow mom was offering sympathy and asking questions about my son's diagnosis. I was so very tired, I could barely put two coherent sentences together in a row, but I was doing my best. Then I heard her say something that I was surprised to find myself wince at a bit. I won't repeat it because the last thing any of us need to do is start examining other people's words for tone perfection or raking them over the coals for how supposedly insensitive they are. I will say that, having the advantage of distance and (hopefully) a bit of maturity, I can see now that she was trying very much to be sensitive. But, nevertheless, I was offended—hurt even. I started storing up this tale of woe to tell my husband. Thankfully, by the time he and I had the chance to talk, the Lord had already dealt with me, and while I did share the conversation with him, it wasn't as a tale of personal woe but as a way God had humbled me to receive imperfect (but still loving) words from a fellow sister in Christ. Hers weren't the words I would have preferred, but they were no reason to indulge self-pity.

Being the mom of a special needs son means that my opportunities for woundedness since that time haven't shrunk; they've grown—they're as readily available as mosquitoes in a Minnesota summer. I can be hurt when my son isn't included in something, hurt

that people with disabilities suffer indignities, hurt by how some don't "get it," and a hundred other things. But all those reactions don't say as much about my situation as they do about my heart.

SEEKING THE FOOD OF FLATTERY

Flattery is food that tastes dainty and refined when we're receiving it, like those cookies with the special glacé icing, but it always leaves us over-sugared and a bit suspicious. You notice Jesus is about as far from a flatterer as they come. He never even approaches what could be conceived of as flattery. He has this way of always saying it exactly like it is. He's gentle when gentleness is called for; he's unflinchingly direct and full of rebukes when the shoe fits; he's silent before his accusers; in all things, he is truthful and loving.

When I think back to the conversation with the sister in Christ that made me wince, part of what caused the wince was a sense that what I really needed to hear was how great I was in the midst of a trial. I feel fairly certain that had she said something like, "You're such an amazing mom," or, "It's incredible how you're managing all this," I wouldn't have winced in the slightest. I may have deflected the praise—I'm not sure—but I am sure that flattering words go down into the innermost parts without any work or wincing at all. When you start listening for flattery in conversations between women, you'll begin

to notice that they are rife with it. Some relationships wouldn't exist at all except for the mutual flattery that is offered up under the banner of "support" or "encouragement." This ought to have us asking, *what is the difference between flattery and encouragement?* And, *do I have any relationships that are dependent on flattery as their food?*

According to the Scriptures, flattery comes out of a duplicitous person who doesn't have regard for the truth but is seeking the social capital that's gained by making another person feel good. Encouragement, on the other hand, is when one person strengthens another person in the Lord. Flattery often involves compliments that puff a person up *irrespective of the Lord* and ultimately for the benefit of the flatterer; encouragement makes people strong and gives them greater confidence and *trust in the Lord* and how he's working in and through them. This doesn't make every compliment flattery. It's possible to say, "I like your haircut," or, "Cute shoes!" and not be a flatterer. Remember that sin is a heart issue first and foremost. But, nevertheless, compliments are the handmaiden of flatterers.

INSULT OR INVITATION?

The Gospel of Mark tells a tale of true woe. A Gentile woman, Syrophoenician by birth, seeks out Jesus who has "entered a house and did not want anyone to know" (Mark 7:24). Yet this woman finds him and falls down at his feet. Her small daughter had an unclean spirit, and she begs him to cast the demon out of her daughter (Mark 7:24–26). But he puts her off with these words: "Let the children be fed first, for it is not right to take the children's bread and throw it to the dogs" (Mark 7:27). Such a jarring response! This doesn't sound like the Jesus who was so frequently moved with compassion when he saw those in need.

What did Jesus mean by this response? Well, from his own mouth we hear him telling her that he had come for the lost sheep of Israel (Matt. 15:24). His mission was first to feed the Jewish people, not the Gentile people. If we put on a mindset that's quick to be wounded or lusts for flattery, we would read that with shock and horror. He called the woman and her small daughter "dogs"! How could he? The little girl was suffering and the mother was in anguish! We might quickly start to tinker with the text or make excuses for Jesus to make it all a bit less offensive to our ears.

But let's take off that wounded mindset and put on the mindset of humility, the mindset that this Gentile woman brought with her to Jesus. This woman knew something very precious and valuable. She knew that Jesus could help her. She knew he was able to heal her daughter. When she begs him for help, she isn't concerned about what anyone thinks of her. She isn't hurt or downcast when Jesus acknowledges the significant difference between them as Jew and Gentile. She knows the two most important things: she is in need of help, and he is able to give it. That's why she is so bold as to say in response to him, "Yes, Lord, yet even the dogs eat the crumbs that fall from their masters' table" (Matt. 15:27). She agrees with his assessment of her. She enters his metaphor without offense—she is no more than a dog under the table. It is her humility and faith that give her the eyes to see the blessing of being included in any scene where the Lord Jesus is present, even if as a dog. Oh, for faith like hers! Lord grant us the humility of this dear sister!

HUMBLE HEARTS SEEK HELP, NOT FLATTERY

When we have come to the end of our own resources and truly sense our total lack of ability to save ourselves, when we come face to face with our own need, we are in the only place where we can rightly come to Jesus. We bring nothing but our poverty, our sickness, our uncleanness, and our awful hunger. He brings everything to meet that need. And he stoops so low that even the dogs like us can receive his mercy.

Desperation is a terribly wonderful gift. It's when we're desperate that we stop caring about how we look. Desperation can even strip away our lust for flattery and make us unoffendable when in the presence of God and his people. But desperation doesn't always work to our spiritual advantage—it can also drive us further into ourselves and our sinfulness. It's only when desperation drives us to the scraps under the Lord's table that it produces the fruit of humility and the healing found in the crumbs from Jesus's hand.

There is strength and joy and salvation in those crumbs. There is more power in the tiniest morsel of belief and trust in Jesus than in all the food of flattery to be found in

the world. The world simply doesn't give life. It is serving up feasts of flattery. It is frequently the fuel for the engine called "marketing." It laces advertisements and commercials. It infects friendships and blinds them to any experience of real, Christlike love. We must not gorge ourselves on flattery—either as a flatterer or as one eager to be fed by it. It will give us something—something that tastes quite delicious in the moment—but what it gives does not last and ultimately leads to destruction.

Instead, receive the hard, unflattering words of Jesus when he says, "Let the children be fed first, for it is not right to take the children's bread and throw it to the dogs" (Mark 7:27). Become like the Syrophoenician woman who kneels before him begging for help and saying, "Yes, Lord, yet even the dogs eat the crumbs that fall from their masters' table" (Matt. 15:27). Humility is the only way to delight yourself in the Lord—whether as a dog or a doorkeeper in his house. And most importantly, hear his response: "Jesus answered her, 'O woman, great is your faith! Be it done for you as you desire'" (Matt. 15:28).

Her faith was not misplaced. She did not lust for flattery but sought help that could be found only in the Savior. A humble heart does not always receive physical healing the way the Syrophoenician woman's daughter did, but it does always receive true help. Our son's disability remains. But would that our faith be such that it knows the real prize is Jesus, not merely different circumstances. The real treasure is in calling him Master and Lord and having it be true. He is ours. We are his. His crumbs sustain to the end if we are desperate enough to have them. The reward for that sort of humility is nothing less than full inclusion in his family. It is the inheritance of a son, not a slave; of a daughter, not a dog.

The Gentile woman was humble enough to enter Jesus's metaphor as an unworthy dog, but she departed as a daughter by faith in Christ, "for everyone who exalts himself will be humbled, and he who humbles himself will be exalted" (Luke 14:11). The Lord has a storehouse of blessing and honor for his people—the question is, are we humble enough to enter as unworthy characters in his story, humble enough to beg for crumbs? Will we insist on our own worthiness or will we receive from the hand of the only worthy person to ever walk the earth? It is a damnable "gospel" that tells women that Jesus's love for them—his life, death, and resurrection—is the proof of their worthiness. Heaven help us! It is the proof of *his* worthiness, not ours. That he would take thought for us! It is the way we come to walk in a manner worthy of *him*.

Oh, sisters, the world, the flesh, and the devil are all conspiring to flatter you right out of God's kingdom. They want you puffed up with high thoughts of your worthiness—but I beg you to take the narrow, low road. Even lower still. He brings us low because we cannot have him any other way. "Stoop, stoop! It is a low entry to go in at heaven's gates."[21]

Discussion Questions

1. Are you easily offended? Do you rely on flattery to grease the wheels of conversation, either as the receiver of flattery or the giver of flattery?

2. Put yourself in the place of the Syrophoenician woman. How would your heart respond to being compared to a dog? Are you more interested in the salvation Jesus provides or being spoken to in a way that you find palatable?

3. Will you humble yourself before the Lord and receive his help and inheritance as his daughter by faith?

PERFECT POPOVERS

5 tablespoons (76 grams)
melted butter

2 eggs

1 cup (240 grams) milk

1 teaspoon
(4 grams) sugar

1 teaspoon (6 grams) salt

1 cup (130 grams)
all-purpose flour

*makes twelve small popovers
or six large popovers[22]*

Preheat the oven to 425 degrees.

Using a 12-cup muffin tin or a 6-cup popover tin (popover tins are larger than muffin tins), drizzle about a teaspoon of butter into each cup or 2 teaspoons into each cup of the 6-cup tin. Combine the eggs, milk, sugar, salt, and 1 tablespoon of butter. Whisk together, beating in the flour a little bit at a time.

Put the muffin tin or popover tin with drizzled butter in each cup into the oven for about 2 minutes or until the butter is sizzling.

Remove the tin from the oven and fill each cup about halfway with the batter (this is true for the 12-cup tin or the 6-cup tin.

Bake for 15–20 minutes at 425 degrees. Reduce the heat to 350 and bake for another 15 minutes or until puffy. Do not open the oven while the popovers are baking.

Serve hot.

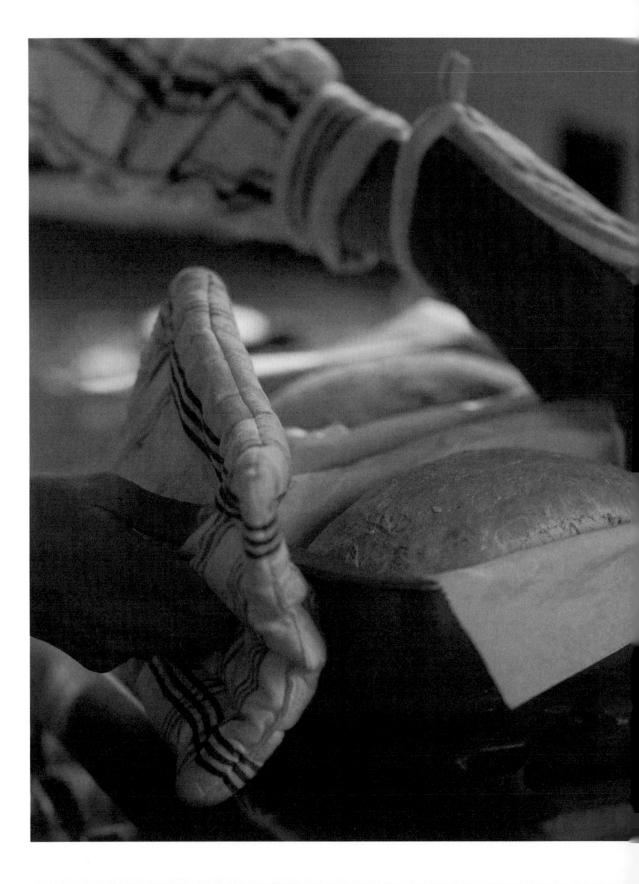

8

Baking in Discipleship

And as they were eating, he took bread, and after blessing it broke it and gave it to them, and said, "Take; this is my body."

MARK 14:22

My husband, Tom, initiated family Bible time when our oldest kids were very little. We both had positive thoughts about family devotions and little experience with them. Thankfully, he took the lead and ordered a book that worked through the Old Testament and provided some discussion questions. We began plodding through it at the end of supper each night. Like most theoretical good ideas, there was a grittiness to actually doing it that we didn't foresee. But there was also a glory that I couldn't have predicted. It was (and continues to be) both a wondrous success and a horrible disaster.

Some nights there would be bickering, fighting, and rude behavior—and that was just the kids! My petty and often self-righteous parental responses dwarfed any childish misbehaviors they were taking up. Then there were my incessant suggestions that Tom do things just a bit differently than he was doing them. *Maybe if we tried starting while the kids were still eating . . . Maybe if you didn't pray quite so long . . . Maybe if the questions were framed differently . . .* He soldiered on, making adjustments here and there, even as I realized that my constant evaluating was ruining my own ability to listen to and receive the word, making me vaguely miserable and a poor example to our children.

Other nights it seemed like glory had descended from on high. The kids understood the word and engaged with us and each other, hearts were soft all around, and spontaneous singing and worship erupted. We were being knit to the word of God and to each other through these small efforts. We left the table with full, thankful tummies and souls.

Jesus taught his disciples some of the deepest truths over supper, not just in the synagogue. He perfectly obeyed and fulfilled Deuteronomy 6:4–7:

> *Hear, O Israel: The Lord our God, the Lord is one. You shall love the Lord your God with all your heart and with all your soul and with all your might. And these words that I command you today shall be on your heart. You shall teach them diligently to your children, and shall talk of them when you sit in your house, and when you walk by the way, and when you lie down, and when you rise.*

As Jesus walked from town to town, he taught his disciples diligently. As they got in a boat and sat in the grass, as they pushed through crowds and prayed in desolate places, as they lay down and rose up, Jesus baked discipleship into everything they did.

Like our unwieldy, yet at times glorious, family Bible times, Jesus had mixed results in the responses from his disciples too. They were tired, they were irritable, they were hungry, they were confused, they were scared, and they were bickering with one another. Also they were following, they were believing, they were amazed, they were participating, and they were his. Surely we can chuckle that at the very last meal Jesus ever spent with them—a meal of epic importance—they begin disputing about who was the greatest among them! How utterly human. It's one good reason (among many) to trust the Bible's historicity. Nobody who was trying to write a convincing fiction about a man who was God would make his chosen disciples so completely normal, so annoyingly like us. But Jesus was committed to sharing life with these men and taking every opportunity to teach them the ways of the kingdom. Their occasional hard-heartedness was not an indication that he was failing at his mission.

BRINGING PEOPLE INTO GOD'S PRESENCE

Rewind with me to the time of the exodus. Outside the Most Holy Place was the sanctuary or Holy Place, where only priests were allowed. God commanded that twelve loaves be set on a table there (Ex. 25:30). These loaves represented the twelve tribes of Israel and were called the "Bread of the Presence," "which means bread that has been set before the Lord's face."[23] They were to be an offering to the Lord and could be eaten only by priests because they were considered holy (Lev. 24:5–9).[24]

And what, or rather who, does that remind us of? How can we not think of God's Son, Immanuel, God with us—the one who became a man and whose presence dwelt with us? The one who lived before the face of the Lord perfectly in all he did. The one who was himself an offering for us, holy and acceptable to God, yet punished for our sin. The one who tells us that he is the bread who gives life to his people—his people made holy by him, a kingdom of priests.

This is the ground of discipleship. It is that we bring people to the bread of the presence. In their encounter with us, they encounter the Lord Christ. Walking alongside others to bring them up in the Lord is the fight for fellowship—not mainly fellowship with one another but mutual fellowship with God. Whose presence is most prominent? There can be no nurturing of the faith of other Christians if the presence of the Lord is not more weighty and real than the presence of one another.

BECOMING A FORK IN THE ROAD

Every day, every hour, we are presented with scads of choices. It could be as little as, "Shall we watch this movie tonight or that one?" or as big as, "Shall I marry this man or not?" In each and every choice, we are offered liberty by the Lord, but not worldly liberty, which is the freedom to do whatever our darkened hearts desire. Instead we are offered a much freer and more costly liberty; that is, when presented with sin or righteousness, we are free to do what's right. Joe Rigney says, "Our little decisions, when gathered together, turn out to be not so little after all. We are always sowing seeds of our future selves."[25]

When we take on the task of making disciples of Jesus, we become the occasion for a fork in the road in the lives of others. Our mere presence forces them to make a decision. This is not because we are perpetually confrontational but because holiness is rarely neutral. When a friend is trying to make a choice about which movie to watch—one being trashy and the other decent—you don't have to launch into ten reasons why you won't watch the trashy one, but your simple resolve not to watch it forces her to either depart from your fellowship or maintain it.

We carry Christ within everywhere we go. This means that his holy presence is with us. This ought to make us willing to be the fork in the road like he was in his earthly life. Whether in a conversation moving toward gossip, or a good time taking a turn toward bad jokes, or whatever the situation, we have the privilege of creating a fork in the road for others. If it doesn't seem like a privilege but rather as something terribly uncomfortable, that's because of course it is, but it's also a surprising path to profound fellowship with the Lord and others.

When I was nineteen years old, that perfect age where one has the confidence of someone much older but the lack of awareness of someone much younger, I was put in a momentarily difficult situation. A man several years older made an inappropriate comment to me after church. Rather than smile or let it slide, I objected to what he said. Little did I know that my future husband was a short distance away observing this scene. Tom and I weren't dating and didn't really know each other at the time. But he loves to tell the story of watching my forthright and direct response in the face of this older man's foolishness as *the event* that attracted him to me. Well, that and the chocolate swirl pie I brought to Bible study, but I digress.

I have always felt terribly embarrassed when he recounts that scene because of how young and bold I was. But looking back, I can see the fork in the road that was created by the conviction of Christ's Spirit in me and my willingness to act on it. Not only did it create a fork in the road for the man with the inappropriate comment, but, unbeknownst to me, it also did for another man who was watching from the sidelines.

This same type of situation is played out hundreds and thousands of times in all our lives. We are always in places where we are called to be Christ's presence. When we respond in accordance with Christ's Spirit, everyone around us is affected. They are either repelled or drawn in, challenged or comforted, softened or hardened. This is the fork in the road that alienates and reconciles—it is the bread of Jesus's presence. John Frame says:

> In Scripture, even in the OT, table fellowship with God is an important element of the covenant blessing. When two people are at odds with each other, they need to be reconciled. Reconciliation can, of course, be rather superficial. But when it is deep and profound, when it is complete reconciliation, not only do you become friends again with your former enemy, but you have him to dinner.[26]

We live in a world at odds with the presence of Christ, which means it is at odds with us as well. Yet we have a reconciling ministry to perform. When we allow ourselves to be the fork in the road, as uncomfortable as it may be, we are giving the people around us an opportunity to be reconciled to God. We are asking them to come with us, to be in fellowship with us around his table. We are inviting them into his presence.

WORDS FOR WOMEN

Being a follower of Jesus is one reality with more than one expression. I would be remiss to write a whole book urging you to read and receive *all* of God's word but leave off some of the particulars aimed at women. Our God is not vague or generic. He is a God of detail and order. He attends to the fine print. Many don't care for that, because it leaves us no room to hide. When I tell my child to go upstairs and clean her room, that's vague enough for all kinds of interpretations, but if I tell her to go upstairs, pick up all the clothes off her floor, put them away, straighten her nightstand, make her bed, vacuum, dust, and put the closet back in order—she's in for it. There's no pretending not to know what I was expecting.

God, while not any sort of micromanaging taskmaster, does give us instructions so that none of us can say back to him, "Well, I just didn't know what you were expecting of me, Lord." He's specific and clear. He says this in regard to his expectations for women and discipleship in the church:

> Older women likewise are to be reverent in behavior, not slanderers or slaves to much wine. They are to teach what is good, and so train the young women to love their husbands and children, to be self-controlled, pure, working at home, kind, and submissive to their own husbands, that the word of God may not be reviled. (Titus 2:3–5)

This brief passage among all sixty-six books of the Bible, small as it may be, is impossible for us to ignore, at least not if we care to have one whiff of internal honesty. It's impossible to ignore because it is so simple and clear. There are no exegetical difficulties, no hard-to-understand Greek words that we can take cover under—nothing. Just the plain word of God addressed directly to us women.

But I'm hoping that you'll agree with me that there is nothing in this passage that we want to run away from! Have you ever considered how terrible the opposite of this passage would be? What if God told us to be irreverent, slanderers, and alcoholic slaves to wine? What if it was our job to teach bad things, to break up marriages, and make excuses for loveless, neglectful mothering? What if we were urging women to be out of control, impure, lazy in their homes, unkind, and rebellious toward their husbands? Does that have any appeal? I hope not!

I don't want to dodge any of your real questions though. Some of you might be wondering why women's discipleship includes teaching women to be workers at home. You may also be hung up on that part about "submissive to their own husbands." Would you think with me for a minute about your body?

WHY OUR BODIES MATTER IN DISCIPLESHIP

The existence of my female body is part of God's communication to me. It tells me what I can and cannot do. It sets me on a trajectory in life. The ontological reality of my body makes some pursuits fitting and others unfitting. Because of my body, I can be wife, not husband, mother, not father, sister, not brother, daughter, not son. Because of my body, I have the potential to nurture and grow life inside of me and outside of me.

Our bodies speak commands, *shalls* and *shall nots,* as authoritative as the direct commands in Scripture from the mouth of God. The commands inherent in our bodies also come from God's mouth, for it was God who formed and made our bodies—God who breathed life into them. What he has shaped and fashioned as male and female is an irrevocable statute. No matter how we might try to change our bodies, the deeper realities of chromosomes and DNA cannot lie. They speak what God tells them to speak.

The plain teaching of our bodies also extends into areas of *oughtness*. For example, men generally ought to physically protect women and children; women generally ought to take particular care for young ones. Why? Because men generally have larger and stronger bodies, and women generally have bodies made to nurture young life—and with the Creator's design come emotional and psychological fittedness as well. So when Paul speaks his instructions to older women and younger women, we shouldn't be surprised. Submission is fitting in relation to our bodies. Making home a priority is fitting for the woman, whose body has the potential to be a home. There is a design at work, and it is not arbitrary but profoundly good.

But if you say, "I'm not married and I don't have kids! Does all this still apply?" Well, yes and no. Are you to be submissive to your nonexistent husband? Of course not! That's silly. But don't let that fact excuse you from being the sort of woman who would be submissive to her husband if she had one. You might think, *Well what on earth would that look like?* And lest you get any weird ideas, I don't mean you ought to go around

practicing submission to random guys your age. Quite the contrary—submission of a wife to a husband is meaningful because it only exists *inside* the marriage.

If you want to know if you would be the kind of woman who is submissive to her husband if she had one, then simply check to see whether you're the kind of woman who submits to God's word. When God says that older women are to teach what is good to younger women, including self-control, purity, love, and submission, are you eager to obey that command to teach as the older woman? You don't have to be married to help teach and train the married women that they ought to love their children and submit to their own husbands. Do you want to learn from women who are older than you, or perhaps not older, strictly speaking, but wiser and more mature in some area? Are you the kind of woman whose life prevents the word of God from being reviled? That's the kind of woman Titus 2 seeks to produce. It is a beautiful thing that God ordained women to have such a prominent role in the maturation and discipleship of other women. He knows what he's doing. He wants women to bring the presence and weightiness of God to bear in the nitty-gritty realities of each other's lives.

Discipleship is often not a straight line. We walk with people, we teach them what we know of God's word and ways, we bring the presence of the Lord to bear in their everyday moments, and sometimes they receive it and other times they don't. Their progress is slow, and sometimes ours is slower. If we aren't frustrated with others' lack of growth, we're discouraged by our own. Yet discipleship is not a ten-step program to glory; it is not a quick fix or a fixer-upper. We are disciples making disciples. We can take heart that God has made both the formal and the informal bits of our everyday lives the places of discipleship. From the sermon to the car ride home, from baptism to washing the car, from the Lord's Supper to lunch at the ball game—the bread of the presence is Jesus, and there's never a time when he is not with us.

Discussion Questions

1. What ways can you bake in discipleship to the normal rhythms of life? How does Titus 2:3–5 factor into who and how you disciple others?

2. How can you bring Christ's presence to bear in the relationships God has given you?

3. Are you willing to be a fork in the road in the lives of others as you invite them to walk with the Lord?

EVERYDAY COTTAGE BREAD

This is wonderful sandwich bread that every child loves to eat.[27] It is the perfect PB&J bread. I included a sourdough version for those of you keeping your sourdough starter on hand for such a time as this.

6½ cups (780 grams) all-purpose flour

1 tablespoon (17 grams) instant yeast

1½ tablespoons (13 grams) brown sugar

1½ tablespoons (21 grams) melted butter

2⅔ cups (624 grams) warm milk

1 tablespoon (17 grams) salt

makes two loaves

In a large bowl whisk the flour, yeast, and sugar.

Add the melted butter, warmed milk, and salt.

Mix with a spoon or dough hook (manually or with a stand mixer) until it's combined (it may look shaggy) and let it rest for 20 minutes.

Turn out the dough on a counter and knead for 10 minutes, adding more flour if necessary to make a dough that is tacky but not sticky.

Put the dough in large bowl and let it rise until doubled in size. This should take approximately an hour or more.

Once the dough has doubled, turn it out on the counter and divide it into two equal pieces. Shape the dough into loaves and put them in greased loaf pans. You can also line the loaf pans with parchment.

Cover the loaf pans with a damp towel and let the dough rise for another 30 minutes to 1 hour. Preheat the oven to 375 degrees.

Bake at 375 for 35–40 minutes. The internal temperature should be 200 degrees. Let the bread cool on a cooling rack.

100 PERCENT SOURDOUGH COTTAGE BREAD

2⅔ cups (630 grams) warm milk

1½ tablespoons (14 grams) melted butter

1 cup (250 grams) leaven (this is the sourdough starter that has been refreshed with at least 100 grams flour and 100 grams water the night before)

6¼ cups (780 grams) all-purpose unbleached flour

1 tablespoon (15 grams) salt

1½ tablespoons (15 grams) brown sugar

makes two loaves

Pour the warm milk and melted butter into a large mixing bowl.

Place the bowl on a kitchen scale and tare to 0. Pour in 200 grams of leaven. The leaven should float. Mix in the leaven with your hands until it is dissolved in the milk.

Add the flour, salt, and sugar. Mix with a spoon or dough hook (manually or with a stand mixer) until it's combined (it may look shaggy) and let it rest for 20 minutes.

Turn out the dough on a counter and knead it for 10 minutes, adding more flour if necessary to make a dough that is tacky but not sticky.

Put the dough in a large bowl and let it rise until doubled in size. This should take approximately 3–5 hours. If you want to speed up the process, you can turn your oven into a proofing drawer by turning it on at 350 degrees for 1 minute, then turning it off and putting the dough in the warm environment.

Once the dough has doubled, turn it out on the counter and divide it into two equal pieces.

Shape the dough into loaves and put it in greased loaf pans. You can also line the loaf pans with parchment.

Cover the loaf pans with a damp towel and let the dough rise for another 2–3 hours. Preheat the oven to 375 degrees.

Bake at 375 for 35–40 minutes. The internal temperature should be 200 degrees. Let the bread cool on a cooling rack.

9

Kneaded and Shaped
by Every Word

And after fasting forty days and forty nights, he was hungry. And the tempter come and said to him, "If you are the Son of God, command these stones to become loaves of bread." But he answered, "It is written, 'Man shall not live by bread alone, but by every word that comes from the mouth of God.'"

MATTHEW 4:2–4

G od interprets himself and his actions. When the Israelites had been led through the wilderness for forty years, God made sure to remind them through Moses of what he'd been doing: "[God] humbled you and let you hunger and fed you with manna, which you did not know, nor did your fathers know, that he might make you know that man does not live by bread alone, but man lives by every word that comes from the mouth of the LORD" (Deut. 8:3). He gives them a summary of *why* he did it: God let them hunger and fed them with manna so that they would learn to live by his every word. The manna was a way of teaching them that their provision was from God's mouth, not from themselves.

Jesus quotes this verse to Satan while he's being tempted in his own wilderness (Matt. 4:4). One thing I regularly give thanks for (and invite you to give thanks for as well), is the specificity of the word *every*. We live by *every* word that comes from the mouth of the Lord. We don't live by just some of the words from his mouth, not just the New Testament, or the Epistles, or the parts of Scripture that tell us the explicit gospel, or the sections that are especially fun to memorize, or the places that make for good quips and have that uplifting lilt to them, but by every single word. And that ought to make us eager to actually have read every single word—to actually know all the words that are coming from his mouth.

But assuming that you have read his word, or are reading it, or are at least eager to do so more if you haven't yet read as much as you desire, we must also consider this crucial point: what does it mean to *live* by every word?

GATHERING INGREDIENTS BUT NOT USING THEM

Imagine you have a wonderful recipe for chocolate croissants in front of you. You know it's wonderful because it has hundreds of five-star reviews, and the pictures that accompany it show gorgeous laminated dough baked to flaky, tender perfection. You begin

captive those who were their captors, and rule over those who oppressed them.

When the LORD has given you rest from your pain and turmoil and the hard service with which you were made to serve, ⁴you will take up this taunt against the king of Babylon:

"How the oppressor has ceased, the insolent fury ceased! The LORD has broken the staff of the wicked, the scepter of rulers, that struck the peoples in wrath with unceasing blows, that ruled the nations in anger with unrelenting persecution.

The whole earth is at rest and quiet; they break forth into singing. The cypresses rejoice at you, the cedars of Lebanon, saying, 'Since you were laid low, no woodcutter comes up against us.'

10 Sheol beneath is stirred up to meet you when you come; it rouses the shades to greet you, all who were leaders of the earth; it raises from their thrones all who were kings of the nations. All of them will answer and say to you: 'You too have become as weak as we! You have become like us!'

11 Your pomp is brought down to Sheol, the sound of your harps; maggots are laid as a bed beneath you, and worms are your covers.

12 "How you are fallen from heaven, O Day Star, son of Dawn! How you are cut down to the ground, you who laid the nations low! ¹³You said in your heart, 'I will ascend to heaven; above the stars of God...

I will set my throne on high...
I will sit on the mount of assembly in the far reaches of the north;
I will ascend above the heights of the clouds...

gathering the ingredients and the necessary tools: bread flour, yeast, poolish, butter, salt, rolling pin, parchment paper, dough hook, milk, water, dark chocolate bars, more butter, etc. You read the recipe closely, trying to understand and envision every step. You read it again. Then you read it a third time. You double check your ingredients and tools. You read more about the ingredients themselves and how they interact with each other. You put them all in a neat row on the counter in the order in which they will need to be mixed. You make sure your stand mixer is plugged in.

Your husband or friend or child comes in and asks, "Hey, whatcha up to?" And you reply, "Oh, come see! I made chocolate croissants today!" He says, "That's wonderful! Can I try one?"

Of course he can't try one because you didn't actually make chocolate croissants. You thought about making them, you got everything ready to make them, you even learned about what it would require to make them, but you didn't actually do it. Your hands are still clean, your apron unsoiled, your ingredients have not been mixed together. They're just sitting there—each on its own—doing nothing.

This is the way too many of us fake ourselves out into thinking we're all good when it comes to following Christ. We have the ingredients ready. We've read the instructions three times in a row. We sound really knowledgeable about chocolate croissants, but when it comes down to it, we've never actually made them. So we give lots of smart-sounding advice to other Christians, Christians who actually do have their hands in the dough and are trying to incorporate their butter block before it starts melting. We're faking it really well; we may have even convinced ourselves that our familiarity with the recipe is a substitute for actually following it—that *envisioning* how good it would be is the same thing as having *tasted* it.

But mere theoretical eating of a wonderfully layered chocolate croissant is depressing (among other things) and isn't remotely close to actually eating one.

THE CHASM BETWEEN LIVING BY EVERY WORD AND MERELY KNOWING THE WORDS

A great chasm separates those who merely have all the ingredients lined up on the counter, have examined each one, and know the recipe frontward and back, and those who have put all the ingredients together in a bowl and are kneading the dough, working the yeast through every part of it, and are on their way to making actual food (even if they're a smidge fuzzy on all the details). On one side of the chasm is a life lived by every word that proceeds from God's mouth, and on the other side are really astute-sounding fakes. It's the difference between knowing about a thing and knowing a thing.

God wants us to live by every word that comes from his mouth, which is different from merely knowing all the words. He wants us to *live* by them—that means to receive them, to trust them, to bank everything on them, to count them more precious than our own thoughts, and to obey them with every fiber of our being.

You might be wondering, *How do I know if I'm living by the words of the Lord or if I merely know them really well?* One good diagnostic question is, How do you respond when things don't go the way you want? When we don't get our own way, we have an opportunity to assess whether we've merely read the recipe or whether we've tried it out. We can even see that in the verse from Deuteronomy: God *humbled* the Israelites and *let them hunger* so that they would learn to live by his every word. Did the Israelites want to be humbled and hungry? No way. Being denied what we want humbles us. It reminds us that we aren't in control, which in turn reveals to us whether we are content and comforted by the fact that *God* is in control. Elisabeth Elliot said, "If God is in control of the big things, He must also be in control of the little ones."[28]

What's fascinating about Elliot's words is that our modern mindset likely also needs to hear the inverse of them. Many Christians can embrace Jesus as their personal friend, the one who cares about them on an intimate level. We find a close parking spot at Walmart and think that the Lord must be winking at us today—everything is going just the way we want. "It's a God-thing" when the person in front of us pays for our drive-up coffee. But when a global pandemic hits, we refuse to entertain ideas that he might be sovereign over it and working his purposes through it. Perhaps what we need to be reminded of is this: if God is in control of the little things, he must also be in control of the big ones.

"Every word of God proves true," whether in regard to a pandemic or a parking spot, a prophecy from Scripture coming to pass or proverbial wisdom to guide our steps (Prov. 30:5). Not only that, God says, "so shall my word be that goes out from my mouth; it shall not return to me empty, but it shall accomplish that which I purpose, and shall succeed in the thing for which I sent it" (Isa. 55:11). God's words are not vain; they are not empty; they are not false. They are true from the tiniest detail of your everyday minutiae to the biggest events in history. They shape and fashion; they cause and create. We *live* by God's words, both in this world he has spoken into existence and also in the words of his book.

THE PAIN AND PURPOSE OF KNEADING AND SHAPING

I actually have made chocolate croissants a number of times. The last recipe I tried was new to me. It was from a famous bakery and was more complicated than the previous way I'd done it. I had a feeling the results would be quite a bit better, but it took some deep breaths and multiple read-throughs before I decided to go for it. I began mid-morning on the Saturday before Easter Sunday and around ten o'clock that night, I was still in the kitchen desperately trying to roll out the laminated dough to the correct size. My feet hurt, my arms ached, and I was tired and stressed. It sounds so silly! I was making croissants, not negotiating world peace.

Nevertheless, those particular croissants were hard work. The recipe *was* better than the others I'd made, and because of that, it required more of me—more time, more mental work, more physical work, just generally more. It also gave me more—more layers, more deliciousness, more satisfaction with the end result, more delight on the faces of my loved ones when they bit into them. And like those particular croissants, we Christians also require a lot of work.

Will you shift metaphors with me? Rather than view yourself as the baker who has finally decided to get in the game and make the croissants, not just ruminate about them, picture yourself as the dough. God is the baker. He's the one doing the kneading and shaping. He's the one grabbing the dough, pressing down with a fair bit of weight, turning it, and pressing down again. He's the one making sure it rolls out to the proper rectangular size. He's the one cutting the dough, rolling it, and baking it in his own 500-degree oven. This means you're the one being pressed on, turned, and pressed on again. You're the one being rolled out, cut and formed, and popped in a blistering oven. That is to say, you're the one being transformed by the master baker. All that kneading and shaping, the rolling and stretching, is more akin to pain than pleasure, is it not?

Knowing there is a purpose behind the pressing down and rolling out can change our experience of the pain. When we don't get our way in life, we have comfort in the knowledge that God's ways are better and always go according to plan. And here is where I confess to you that I cannot understand the trend of trying to comfort those experiencing unwanted circumstances by telling them that God had nothing to do with their difficulties. But that is cold comfort indeed. How can there be comfort in believing that there is no plan in the pain? What love can be discerned from a God who just lets things happen with no good reason? Where is the hope in that futility? And these theoretical questions are putting aside the simple reality that God himself tells us there certainly is a purpose in our pain and suffering and circumstances—and *he means it to comfort us.* Persecution, trials, unjust pain (which is often code for "when other people sin against you") are things the Scriptures anticipate for us in order to comfort us with God's sovereignty when they actually happen.

Dear readers, we know the character of our God. We know that he is a Father to his children. We know that he does not give stones when asked for bread, or serpents when asked for fish (Matt. 7:9–10). How do we know? Because every word of his has proved true. He did what he said he would—the Messiah has come, the good news has been

declared to the poor, the captives are set free in Christ, the root of Jesse has sprouted. Jesus suffered and died and was raised to life on the third day, just as he said. Every word of the Lord proves true. He *promises* and *guarantees* that he will grant eternal life to all those who believe in the Lord Jesus, all those who put their hope in his word. We can trust that promise because he's kept all the others!

Therefore, we have the greatest comfort imaginable when things don't go our way: we have *his word* that he is working it all for our good in ways beyond our finding out in the here and now. We don't need a chart outlining each and every purpose; we just need to be able to trust the heart and word of God. We need to remember that he does indeed have good purposes—one of which is most undoubtedly our transformation into his likeness, which is to say, our holiness.

It is in those horrid times of suffering that we discover whether or not we live by every word that comes from God's mouth. Do we really believe that God is for us in Christ? Can we lean hard on the words of the Savior, who calls himself gentle and lowly and beckons us to come to him for rest? Will we go ahead and take up his easy yoke, or will we simply stare at it from afar? Will we remember that it is not God's mission to protect us from the very things that are his most potent tools in shaping us into his Son's likeness? It is not his mission to spare us all pain but rather to ensure that every ounce of it is ripe with good purpose. This is our God. We can bank our lives on the words that come from his mouth. We can endure the kneading and shaping, the pressing down and turning over, when we know it's coming directly from his loving hand.

Discussion Questions

1. How do you respond when things don't go the way you want? Do you turn to God's word or away from it?

2. What would it look like for you to start banking on God's words—truly living by them even in the midst of pain or difficulty?

3. How does God's plan to send his Son to die on a cross for our sin and be raised to new life reframe what it means for us to live by God's words?

CHOCOLATE CROISSANTS

Pluck up your courage, friends. These croissants are hard, but that means they're also exceptionally good.[29] They are adapted from the incomparable Tartine Bread *book and are better than what most bakeries produce, and that's the plain truth of the matter.*

POOLISH:

200 grams (1⅓ cups) unbleached all-purpose flour

200 grams (¾ cup) water

3 grams (1 teaspoon) instant yeast

DOUGH (*also called the détrempe*):

450 grams (1¾ cups) whole milk (room temperature or slightly warm)

300 grams (1¼ cups) leaven (see the instructions for Sourdough Starter on page 95 on how to make leaven)

400 grams (1½ cups) poolish

1000 grams (7¾ cups) bread flour

30 grams (1½ tablspoons) salt

2 DAYS BEFORE BAKING:

Refresh your sourdough starter before you go to bed so that you will have leaven the next day.

Also, just before you go to bed, make the poolish by mixing the flour, water, and yeast in a bowl or container. Put in the fridge overnight.

ONE DAY BEFORE BAKING, BEGINNING MID-MORNING OR EARLIER:

Pour the milk into a large mixing bowl. Add the leaven and poolish to the milk (they should both float). Dissolve them into the milk with your hands.

Add the flour, salt, sugar, and yeast. Mix with your hands or a large spoon or a dough hook until all the flour is incorporated.

Let the dough rest for approximately 30 minutes. Stretch and fold the dough. Repeat every ½ hour over the next 1½ hours.

Transfer the dough to plastic wrap or a large plastic bag and press it down into a flat rectangular shape. Put in the fridge for 2–3 hours.

Make the butter block by cutting the cold butter into cubes and placing them in between layers of plastic wrap. Using a rolling pin, pound the butter, incorporating ½ cup of flour as you pound. This should form one cohesive mass. You want the butter block to be cool and firm (not warm!), yet pliable.

recipe and ingredients list continued on page 145

85 grams (6¾ table-spoons) sugar

10 grams (2 teaspoons) instant yeast

BUTTER BLOCK:

400 grams cold, unsalted butter (this is just under four sticks of butter or 31 tablespoons)

60 grams (½ cup) flour

CHOCOLATE FILLING:

85 grams (6 tablespoons) cold unsalted butter

320 grams (2 cups) semi-sweet or dark chocolate chips

EGG WASH:

3 large egg yolks

10 grams (2 teaspoons) heavy cream

turbinado sugar (for sprinkling on top of egg wash)

makes twelve to sixteen croissants

Put the butter block on parchment paper and shape the butter block into an 8x12-inch rectangle. You can store it in the fridge while you continue with the recipe, but you don't want it to get so cold that it isn't pliable enough to be rolled out with the dough.

Put the dough on a heavily floured counter and roll it out to a 12x20-inch rectangle. The long side of the dough should be horizontal, the short side vertical.

Place the butter block on top of the dough so that it's covering two-thirds of the dough. Fold the one-third of the dough that doesn't have butter covering it onto the part covered with it, like you would fold a letter. Then fold the other side with butter onto the center, enclosing the butter inside. Now the dough and butter will be folded in thirds to create layers of dough-butter-dough-butter-dough.

Rotate the dough (with butter block inside) 90 degrees and roll it out to a 12x20-inch rectangle again. This is called the first "turn."

Fold the dough like a letter once more, trying to keep the edges even.

Wrap the dough in plastic wrap and refrigerate it for 1 hour (no more than 1 hour).

Place dough on a heavily floured counter and roll it out to a 12x20-inch rectangle, with the long side horizontal and the short side vertical. This is the second "turn."

Fold the dough like a letter again.

Wrap the dough in plastic wrap and refrigerate it for 1 hour (no more than 1 hour).

Place the dough on a heavily floured counter and roll it out to a 12x20-inch rectangle, with the long side horizontal and the short side vertical. Now you've completed three "turns."

continued on following pages

Your dough should now be 8x12 inches and about 2 inches thick. Wrap the dough in plastic wrap and put it in the fridge for a minimum of 1 hour (it can be left in the fridge for up to a day).

Make the chocolate filling by melting the butter and chocolate together (in a saucepan or microwave). Spread the chocolate on parchment paper (about ½ inch thick) and let it cool to harden.

Line baking sheets with parchment paper.

Place the dough on the floured counter and roll it into an 18x24-inch rectangle that is approximately ½ inch thick. (This is the hardest part, in my opinion.)

Cut the dough in half lengthwise to get two 9x24-inch rectangles.

Using a ruler, make notches along the 24-inch side of the dough at 4-inch intervals. Then, using a knife or pizza cutter, cut the dough into long triangles that are 4 inches long on one side.

Cut the now-hardened chocolate into 3-inch-long bars that are about 1/2 inch in width. Place the chocolate bars on the 4-inch side of the triangle and roll the triangles into croissant shapes with the chocolate inside.

Place the croissants on parchment-lined baking sheets. Cover and put in the fridge overnight.

ON BAKING DAY:

Take the croissants out of the fridge.

Preheat the oven to 425 degrees.

Make the egg wash by whisking the yolks and cream. Brush the tops of the croissants with the wash.

Sprinkle croissants with liberal amounts of turbinado sugar.

Bake at 425 degrees for 30 minutes or until a deep brown.

Enjoy!

10

The Hunger That Remains

Blessed are those who hunger and thirst for righteousness,
for they shall be satisfied.

MATTHEW 5:6

Regular Bible reading is not mainly the *fruit* of the Christian life; it is the *food* of Christian survival.

If you are thinking (whether consciously or subconsciously) that reading your Bible or getting into a Bible study is the proof that you're a Christian—the receipts that can prove your validity to yourself or others—then your relationship with the Bible will likely always be performative and fraught. But when you understand Bible reading as the means, the food, the fuel, the sustenance of your Christian life, then you will consume it with joy, like a hungry person eats bread.

The word *Bethlehem* means "house of bread." Bethlehem was the place Jacob's wife Rachel was buried; it is the place where Samuel anointed David to be king of Israel, the place from where Naomi and her husband fled because the "house of bread" was experiencing famine, the place Naomi and Ruth returned to be provided for in every way, and the place of which Micah prophesied:

> *But you, O Bethlehem Ephrathah,*
> *who are too little to be among the clans of Judah,*
> *from you shall come forth for me*
> *one who is to be ruler in Israel,*
> *whose coming forth is from of old,*
> *from ancient days. (Mic. 5:2)*

Yes, this "house of bread," Bethlehem, was the place where the true bread was born, the Lord Christ. It is also the name of my church, the people of God I gather with in Minnesota. The name is fitting, is it not? God's people are a house of bread. And when the house of bread gathers, we are fed the word of God week after week after week, served to us by faithful men who are holding fast to the trustworthy word as handed down to them by the apostles and the prophets. But bread isn't just for Sundays; we are meant to be a house of bread all week long. Yet how many of us are fasting from Monday

to Saturday, only to have a vague, pathetic appetite come Sunday. It seems when we stop eating, we lose the gift of the hunger that is meant to remain in this life.

A BANQUET OF EXCUSES

There is a saying, "Don't bite the hand that feeds you." From the beginning of time, humanity has been doing just that. It's not that we have actually been able to wound or hurt God by biting at him, but we've been gnawing and angry about his food, his provision, even while we can't take one breath or make our heart beat one thump or chew one morsel of food or produce one ounce of life apart from him.

Jesus says his kingdom is like a great banquet. When one man heard him say this, he responded:

A man once gave a great banquet and invited many. And at the time for the banquet he sent his servant to say to those who had been invited, "Come, for everything is now ready." But they all alike began to make excuses. The first said to him, "I have bought a field, and I must go out and see it. Please have me excused." And another said, "I have bought five yoke of oxen, and I go to examine them. Please have me excused." And another said, "I have married a wife, and therefore I cannot come." So the servant came and reported these things to his master. Then the master of the house became angry and said to his servant, "Go out quickly to the streets and lanes of the city, and bring in the poor and crippled and blind and lame." And the servant said, "Sir, what you commanded has been done, and still there is room." And the master said to the servant, "Go out to the highways and hedges and compel people to come in, that my house may be filled. For I tell you, none of those men who were invited shall taste my banquet." (Luke 14:15–24)

The man assumed that if the Lord was giving a banquet, what a blessing it would be to eat his bread! Yet Jesus shows us that most people don't want his bread and are simply too busy to come and eat it.

As I've walked through different seasons of life, I've noticed that my attitude toward Bible reading and eating the bread of life found in Jesus has had some bumps. I already shared with you the problem I had with scoffing. But there have been other permutations. And I've noticed I'm not the only one. Women often have their own particular banquet of excuses when it comes to reading God's word and eating the bread of life, Jesus Christ. If we get under the surface—beyond bad Bible habits or wrong Bible study methods—there are almost always deeper problems at play that keep us from the very simple act of reading and receiving God's word.

I offer these five types of women to you for your consideration: (1) women in need of a meal, (2) women in need of table fellowship, (3) women in need of digestion, (4) women in need of an appetite, and (5) women enjoying a feast.[30]

WOMEN IN NEED OF A MEAL

Most women today are incredibly busy. Maybe it's a calendar full of events and obligations, or maybe it's simply busyness caring for people at home. Busy nights, busy mornings, busy afternoons, and crazy-busy dinner times. I've got a soft spot for moms of littles especially! You may be so busy that you can't remember to eat lunch. I remember those days. On more than one occasion I'd get to suppertime, and my husband, Tom, would get home from work, and all of a sudden I'd realize that I'd barely eaten all day. I'd have my lunch plate with two bites taken out of whatever lame sandwich I'd made, and I would have missed breakfast altogether. On a good day, I would have had my coffee, but on the worst ones, my coffee cup would be sitting in the microwave, having been reheated for the fourth time, yet I'd never managed a sip.

Tom is a helpful picture of God's love on days like these. I remember him getting home from work and observing my spiraling, low-blood-sugar state of disarray and saying to me, "It looks like you need to sit down for a little while. Why don't you take a break?" Then a few minutes later he'd come over with a plate of food that he'd prepared for me and a drink and just set it in my lap. And I would slowly start to eat. Can you see the Father's love in that kindness?

He could have said to me, "Come on, why didn't you eat today? What's wrong with you? We have a whole refrigerator full of food!" But, instead, he fed me the way Paul spiritually fed the Thessalonians—tenderly and gently. He covered me in grace, and I was restored with a meal.

That picture of the busy mother who has missed a couple meals may very well be where you are spiritually. Your life is full because you are taking care of the very important and needy gifts (e.g., children or aging parents or jobs or fill in the blank) the Lord has given you. You are doing a good thing; you are fulfilling the call that he's placed on your life when he gave you your children or your folks or your job.

And what you need right now is to sit down and receive the pure spiritual milk of the word that God has prepared for you. Your job is not to fret that you haven't eaten yet today but to simply receive what he has for you now, in this moment. Taste and see that he is good. Eat this:

> The LORD is gracious and merciful,
>> slow to anger and abounding in steadfast love.
> The LORD is good to all,
>> and his mercy is over all that he has made. (Ps. 145:8–9)

God's word is a place for receiving. My hope is that if you're tired and hungry, you would stop trying to go without the life and food found in the Bible.

Don't worry about tomorrow either. Just eat what's put before you: that kid's memory verse, that chapter in Romans, those three verses jotted down on a folded-up 3x5 card. God's words are meant to be consumed the same way we eat breakfast, lunch, and dinner—every day. The meals don't need to be fancy. Better a peanut-butter-and-jelly read-through of 1 and 2 Chronicles than no read-through at all. Better to eat up the book of Numbers on the audio Bible app with some confusion and scratching of the head than to avoid it altogether. Better to have chaotic family Bible time over supper each night with distractions and diaper changes and toddlers falling out of chairs and sleepy moms trying to stay alert during prayer time and tentative dads trying to lead their families in something they've never seen modeled and twelve-year-olds being occasionally bored than to give up altogether. Better to have God's word be a daily, regular meal than to ping-pong from feast to famine as you are beholden to whatever is (or isn't) offered in formal study or spoon-fed to you by the famous.

This is a little like securing your own face mask on the airplane before you try to help anyone else. You may think you don't have time, but trust me—you're not helping anyone by going on a spiritual starvation diet. The food is prepared. Eat up.

WOMEN IN NEED OF TABLE FELLOWSHIP

There may be others of you who come to the table regularly to eat the food of the word, but the delight of the meal is gone. You labor to turn the pages of God's word, mired by guilt and shame because what you've done never feels like enough. You've been sitting at the table alone, force-feeding yourself the word. Too often, discouragement comes because we've thought that the Bible is a string of pearls, going from one beautiful saying to the next, to help us in every situation, but when we actually start reading it, we find out that a lot of it is confusing and doesn't seem to speak to our felt needs at all.

When the kids were younger and our family ate supper around the table, and the meal that I'd prepared wasn't a favorite with the littles, the general atmosphere at the table sometimes became sour. Our place of nourishment and fellowship became a place of unhappiness and drudgery. On those occasions, arguing erupted as kids divided into factions over who liked which dish and who didn't. Often we had to work pretty hard to keep our dinner table a joyful place, especially when the meal being served wasn't quite to the taste of everyone. How did we do it? By laughing together. By not sweating the small stuff. By not overloading the plates. By encouraging every step in the right direction with rounds of applause and cheering.

The same is true in Bible reading. Not every meal is a flavor we're used to. We may have to learn to appreciate parts of the Scripture that are hard to understand or the parts that *aren't* too hard to understand but simply rub us the wrong way. This is a

lot easier when we're in fellowship with others and are able to encourage, exhort, and admonish one another on the way. For those with enthusiasm for some of the harder parts—let it spill out with love and bring others along. We're in this together. We're on the same team. We're learning together, and we want to receive *all* of God's word, not just the parts that make us immediately feel good. From Genesis to Revelation, all of God's word is profitable, even if it isn't the string of pearls we thought it was. It's better! There is breadth and depth that is more than just helpful. It is the food of our life; it is the way to know our God.

WOMEN IN NEED OF DIGESTION

The third type are women who have pulled their chairs up to the table and ingested every bit of food that they can get their hands on. They've eaten and eaten and eaten. And they continue to eat until their eyes start to bulge and the food has lost its flavor and potency in their lives. The satisfaction of checking off the checkbox that says, "Read the Bible ten times this year" has become a sorry replacement for the satisfaction of "taste and see that the LORD is good" (Ps. 34:8).

Is it possible that the act of consuming the word could replace the digestion and nourishment of it? We can know so much and even understand a great deal, but has it found its way into our hands and feet and heart? Has it gone into us in order to work its way out of us? Does the intake of the word lead to an output of living and loving that is more like Christ and puts the gospel on display? How easy it is to be a hearer of the word but not a doer of it. Yet how deadly.

Digesting the word of God means letting it work its way into the private crevices and corners of our heart and mind so that we walk away from it changed women. It means putting ourselves truly *under* the word, in full submission to it, not taking it up for study and evaluation on our own terms. If you see yourself in the latter, then the place to start is with repentance. It is an affront to God to make his word our plaything, even if we appear to be great students, and our highlighters are at the ready.

I recently got my master of arts in exegesis and theology. It took a lot of work to earn that title, yet surely we can all agree it's quite a ridiculous hoot if you think about it. The name of the degree seems to get backwards what studying the Bible is *for*—as though I could master the knowledge of God! The goal is not my mastery of the material but the material's mastery of me. Rather than try to master each book of the Bible or conquer more and more Bible studies, we must remember that we don't get hold of the Bible; it takes hold of us. It's important to know and objectively understand what each book of the Bible says, but the reason we want to know it is so that *we* would be molded by it.

Those who are not digesting God's word, who are not truly taking it in to the innermost parts for transformation, are often more concerned with mastering the text than with being mastered by it. Come back to your first love. Remember that Jesus is Lord and that there is great happiness in obeying his word.

WOMEN IN NEED OF AN APPETITE

Some of you might be reading this but not even sure why. You don't have an interest in the word. Maybe you never have, or maybe you used to but now your appetite has completely dried up. You're not thirsty even though you haven't taken a drink in a very long time. Perhaps you've become cynical about the body of Christ or about Christianity in general. If you're honest, you're hanging on by a thread. You're still going through the motions of faith, but you've started to question whether yours is legit. Doubts are your companion.

It's almost like you've got morning sickness (which everyone knows lasts all day) and just the smell of good food sets you off a bit. You know you should eat, but nothing sounds good, and you're afraid you're going to throw up if you try something. There are only a few things you crave to eat, and none of them are the good food from God's word. You are filling up on worldly junk.

My hope is that you would begin to sip and taste again—that even the crumbs of God's word that you've gotten from this book would be like the saltine crackers and Sprite that get you back to eating the meaty nourishment God has prepared for you. It's no small thing to show up, even though your stomach is turning. It's no small thing that you're hanging on, even if barely. It is ordained by the Lord. I'm asking you to set the cynicism aside, to lay off the garbage diet, and to humble yourself before God. We can ask God to be the one to revive our heart since he's the only one powerful enough to do it. We can ask him to awaken desire and an appetite for him. And we can trust that he'll do it, because that's the kind of God he is.

WOMEN ENJOYING A FEAST

The last women I want to address are those who are not weighed down by any of the things I just mentioned. I'm not saying your life is easy or that your intake of the word is perfect or that you have no room to grow. What I'm saying is that you have entered the banquet room with joy. You are feasting at the table. Your heart is receiving, and you are in fellowship with God and his people as iron sharpens iron. You are being transformed as you eat the bread of life. Praise God!

I ask three small things of you. (1) Do not be weirdly embarrassed about your growth. (2) Do not boast in your transformation. Rather, give thanks for it as a gift from God, and turn a profit on it in the lives of those around you. (3) Keep receiving the word and being transformed by it. You will encounter hungry women, busy women, angry women, apathetic women, eager women, cynical women, and women who are playing with God's word rather than receiving it. You have a gift to give them—your love, your cheerleading, at times your rebukes, and most importantly, your *testimony*. You have tasted the goodness of the Lord! You know the satisfaction of the bread of life! Who can you tell? Who can you invite to the table? Who can you send a card full of Scripture and encouragement and prayers? You are a witness to the life found in Jesus because you are *alive*, at the table, eating the food. Testify to how truly good a Savior he is.

DRESSED FOR SERVICE

Of all the places in Scripture that boggle the mind, this picture from the Gospel of Luke of what's to come when Jesus returns ranks high: "Blessed are those servants whom the master finds awake when he comes. Truly, I say to you, he will dress himself for service and have them recline at table, and he will come and serve them" (Luke 12:37). Did you

catch it? He will dress himself for service, the *servants* will recline at the table, and he will serve the servants. Can you imagine being served food by the Lord? I often think of Jesus's statement to his disciples as one of the most incredible in the Bible: "No longer do I call you servants, for the servant does not know what his master is doing; but I have called you friends, for all that I have heard from my Father I have made known to you" (John 15:15).

Yet the scene in Luke goes further. It is a full reversal. It's not the master calling the servant a friend. It is the master becoming a servant to the servants. It is precisely what Jesus did with his own disciples when he broke bread, served them, and washed their feet.

Being served by the Lord humbles the proud, which is why so many refuse it. For his children, for those who know their need, it is life. Dear sister, there is a banquet of blessing, a house of bread, that you've been invited to. The question is, shall you come up with a banquet of excuses? Will you exercise the faux humility of busyness, of work, or of "not wanting to put anyone out"? Jesus came to put himself out for you. He came to go to a lot of trouble for you. We don't come to the feast and say, "Oh, I sure hope this didn't cost you anything, Jesus!" or, "Please don't go to any trouble for little ole me, Lord!" It did cost him! He did take trouble for us! We show our gratitude by receiving all the work he went to on our behalf. We honor him by eating.

> The angel said to me, "Write this: Blessed are those who are invited to the marriage supper of the Lamb." And he said to me, "These are the true words of God." (Rev. 19:9)

An invitation has been sent. A choice lies before you. I urge you with all my heart to come. Come in and sup with him. Be served by your Savior.

Discussion Questions

1. Which type of woman from this chapter most closely describes your relationship with eating God's word?

2. When you consider the massive cost to Jesus of the table that he has set for you, are you humbled and grateful, or are you embarrassed by the great lengths of sacrifice required for the atonement of your sin?

3. What practical steps can you take to begin eating God's word regularly? Who can you invite to the table and testify to about the goodness of God?

BETTER BISCUITS

I like that these biscuits are cut into rectangles—less fussiness trying to use all the dough. And Peter Reinhart, who came up with this recipe, has done a great job merging a tender and flaky biscuit.[31]

2 tablespoons
(29 grams) vinegar

1 cup (227 grams) cold
heavy whipping cream

½ cup (1 stick or
113 grams) cold
unsalted butter

1¾ cups (227 grams)
unbleached all-
purpose flour

1 tablespoon
(14 grams) sugar

2¼ teaspoons (14 grams)
baking powder

¼ teaspoon (1 or 2 grams)
baking soda

½ teaspoon (3 or 4
grams) salt

*makes twelve to
eighteen biscuits*

Put the butter in the freezer for 30 minutes or more.

Whisk the vinegar and cream together, then refrigerate.

Whisk together the flour, sugar, baking powder, baking soda, and salt in a large mixing bowl.

Using a cheese grater, grate the frozen butter into the dry ingredients (use the large holes of the grater).

Using your fingers, mix the butter pieces into the flour, keeping any clumps from forming but not melting the butter.

Add the vinegar and cream from the fridge to the flour and butter. Mix with a large spoon until it all comes together in a ball. Add a little more cream if necessary.

Place the dough on a floured counter. With floured hands, press and shape the dough into a rectangle. Using more flour as needed, roll the dough into a rectangle, about ½-inch thick.

Fold the dough like a letter, one side onto itself, then the other side. Rotate the dough 90 degrees.

Repeat the rolling out to ½-inch thickness and letter folding three more times, adding flour under the dough and on top as necessary.

continued on page 165

Cut the dough into rectangular biscuits, using a knife, pizza cutter, or bench scraper (you could also use a round cutter).

Preheat the oven to 500 degrees.

Transfer the biscuits to parchment-lined baking sheets. Let them sit for 15–30 minutes before baking.

Put the biscuits in the oven and reduce the heat to 450 degrees. Bake for approximately 15–20 minutes, rotating the pan about halfway through.

Let the biscuits cool briefly and serve warm.

11

An Abundance of Glory

He is the radiance of the glory of God and the exact imprint of his nature.

HEBREWS 1:3

I want to ruminate in this final chapter on the idea, the reality, of glory. This seems foolish, does it not? Wouldn't we all be better served if I simply pointed you to C. S. Lewis's *The Weight of Glory* and tread no further? But mine is a book about hunger, bread, Jesus, and the word of God, and each of those compel me to talk about glory. I will risk that there is yet room to say something helpful about it.

THE NATURE OF BREAD

The very first place bread shows up in the Scriptures is in the Lord's response to Adam's sin:

> *To Adam he said,*
> *"Because you have listened to the voice of your wife*
> *and have eaten of the tree*
> *of which I commanded you,*
> *'You shall not eat of it,'*
> *cursed is the ground because of you;*
> *in pain you shall eat of it all the days of your life;*
> *thorns and thistles it shall bring forth for you;*
> *and you shall eat the plants of the field.*
> *By the sweat of your face*
> *you shall eat bread,*
> *till you return to the ground,*
> *for out of it you were taken;*
> *for you are dust,*
> *and to dust you shall return." (Gen. 3:17–19)*

God curses the ground because of Adam's sin, which in turn leads to repercussions for the bread consumption as well. For many of us living in the United States, with inexpensive bread lining the shelves of grocery stores, gas stations, and bakeries, this effect of the curse seems almost nonexistent. This is pure grace, make no mistake—and we ought to marvel at it in gratitude.

But I want to draw your attention to something else. Up until this point, all we know about Adam and Eve's food was that it grew on trees and plants. Here is the first mention of a different sort of food. Bread doesn't grow on trees. You can't get bread in the wild. Bread involves processes. It requires more than one ingredient. It's a cultivated food. Bread is culture, not just fruit. Bread is man's work mingled with God's creation. And here's the case I want to make: bread is glory.

When God makes Eve from Adam's side, she is, like bread, a thing made from a thing made. If Adam is the raw material, Eve is the cultivation. If Adam is man, Eve is the glory of man. I'm not making this up. God says through Paul that "[man] is the image and glory of God but woman is the glory of man. For man was not made from

woman, but woman from man. Neither was man created for woman, but woman for man" (1 Cor. 11:7–9). There are all kinds of wonderful and glorious implications for this reality between men and women—this is a benefit of creation that I'd urge you to explore. But for now, I want us to think about Jesus as bread.

Jesus is not a created thing. He is not like created man or like created woman made from man. As the creed tells us, "We believe . . . in one Lord Jesus Christ, the only Son of God, begotten from the Father before all ages, God from God, Light from Light, true God from true God, begotten, not made; of the same essence as the Father."[32] Yet, nevertheless, the Son of God became a man. The creed continues, "He came down from heaven; he became incarnate by the Holy Spirit and the virgin Mary, and was *made man*."[33] Jesus is God in the form of man—very God of very God—he is the bread of God, God encultured, God enfleshed, God enjoined to creation, God made visible. He is God glorified. "For God, who said, 'Let light shine out of darkness,' has shone in our hearts to give the light of the knowledge of the glory of God in the face of Jesus Christ" (2 Cor. 4:6).

Can you see him with me? Can you see the glory of God? It is Jesus, the bread of life. "He is the radiance of the glory of God and the exact imprint of his nature" (Heb. 1:3). Eve was a thing made of a thing made—the glory of man. Jesus is God unmade of God unmade—God glorified come to us in human form—come to us as bread.

THE GLORY HE MEANS FOR US

It is a dangerous thing to start thinking about our glory. It seems the moment our mortal minds begin to dwell on any sort of glory that involves ourselves, we are tripped up into idolatry, into a lust for praise and human acknowledgment. We begin admiring ourselves as we imagine how admirable we will, at last, be. But it is even more dangerous not to think on it. It is in the thinking on it, the examination of it, that we purify ourselves in the spirit the apostle John intended us to do. Can we fathom a glory prepared for us in which, upon fixing our minds on it, we do not turn into proud devils? I pray we can, for the Lord calls us to do it.

The Bible does more than hint that we will, in fact, be partakers in God's glory. Jesus prays that the glory God has given him would be given to all of us, so that we may be one, just as he and the Father are one (John 17:22). Peter is so bold as to say it like this:

His divine power has granted to us all things that pertain to life and godliness, through the knowledge of him who called us to his own glory and excellence, by which he has granted to us his precious and very great promises, so that through them you may become partakers of the divine nature, having escaped from the corruption that is in the world because of sinful desire. (2 Pet. 1:3–4)

You and me? Called to his glory? Partaking of the divine nature? How can it be? I won't pretend for a moment that I can explain it! I can't and shan't try. But I will state it as fact: you and I and all those who belong to him and are his children are indeed called to his glory, and we shall become partakers of his divine nature. He has guaranteed our glory by the strength of his will and his word (Rom. 8:29–30).

Here we must rely on John, the beloved disciple, to guide us into visions of our future glory: "Beloved, we are God's children now, and what we will be has not yet appeared; but we know that when he appears we shall be like him, because we shall see him as he is. And everyone who thus hopes in him purifies himself as he is pure" (1 John 3:2–3).

How do we ready ourselves for the glory that awaits? We put every shred of our hope in Jesus and the promise that we will be like him. Hoping in God is how we purify ourselves for glory—that time when the dim glass will be removed, the veil forever lifted, the door finally and fully opened, and the commendation, "Well done," received into a pure heart that can bear to hear it without sinning.

Lewis says, "The promise of glory . . . becomes highly relevant to our deep desire. For glory means good report with God, acceptance by God, response, acknowledgment, and welcome into the heart of things. The door on which we have been knocking all our lives will open at last."[34]

If we can begin to imagine ourselves enjoying his praise because it's *from him*, from his mouth, not mainly because it's centered on us, then we will begin to ready ourselves for heaven. This is the inheritance of children. Do away with all notions of complexity and the tortuous need to nail it all to the wall. Beloved, we are God's *children*. The glory that awaits is not mainly for those who can explain it all, having become so grown up they seem to forget the dust from which they were made. It is for those who will receive it like a child. Maturity in the Christian life is greater and greater childlikeness.

THE GLORY OF EATING LIKE A CHILD

Children can be notoriously difficult to please when it comes to food but not when it comes to bread. I'm sure there is an exception out there, but I've never met a child who turns up his nose at a loaf of bread fresh from the oven. They gather round, eager for the first slice, not because of selfishness but because of delight. Mouths full, they can't help but talk about how good it is and immediately begin asking for more. While their manners may not be as refined as some adults prefer, no one could question their genuine appreciation, their joy, and their happiness in the bread. No one has to ask, "Do you like it?" or urge them to say a dutiful "Thank you."

As someone who makes bread a lot, I can tell you the response of happy children eating bread is the very best response. It is the response that brings me, the bread maker, the most pleasure and honor. So it is with the Lord. The more we can forget ourselves and our overbearing manners and simply receive the bread of life with the joy and delight of a child, the more honor God gets. When we are satisfied by his bread, that is, his Son, he is honored and glorified.[35]

I said at the beginning of this book that I wanted to change your diet. I wanted you awash in *spiritual* gluten.[36] But as I finish, I will own to you that that is only part of my goal. The fuller purpose is not that you would merely eat the bread of life but that you

would eat it *as a child*, for it is only children who really can eat it. For as high and lofty as glory is, God makes up for that loftiness by bestowing it only on humble children:

> *At that time the disciples came to Jesus, saying, "Who is the greatest in the king-*
> *dom of heaven?" And calling to him a child, he put him in the midst of them and*
> *said, "Truly, I say to you, unless you turn and become like children, you will never*
> *enter the kingdom of heaven. Whoever humbles himself like this child is the great-*
> *est in the kingdom of heaven." (Matt. 18:1–4)*

The disciples were seeking glory, asking "Who is the greatest?" Jesus's response must have shocked them as it does us. The greatest are those who have refused a particular kind of aging—the kind that leads to cynicism, scoffing, hypocrisy, and pretense—and instead have grown new, childlike, and full of faith. When Eve ate the forbidden fruit, she "grew up" in the worst way. One could say that was the moment she became that deadly sort of adult that cannot enter the kingdom because she has lost her ability to enjoy all the good things that will be there—most especially God himself.[37] When we turn and become children, every bit of life, from the perfect foam of a latte to the delicious warmth of clothes coming out of the dryer, from the piercing truth of Galatians to the unparalleled wisdom of the parables—all of it becomes vibrant and alive with the goodness of our Father. Everything is received as from *him*. We become partakers of wonder, which gets us about as close as we can get to partaking of the divine nature.

Won't you turn and become his child? Won't you taste and see that he is good? Won't you stir up your hunger for him, knowing that it is his good pleasure to satisfy you with himself? Won't you join me in waiting and hoping for the day when all hunger ceases and we will be glorified in his presence?

> *They shall hunger no more, neither thirst anymore;*
>> *the sun shall not strike them,*
> *nor any scorching heat.*
> *For the Lamb in the midst of the throne will be their shepherd,*
>> *and he will guide them to springs of living water,*
> *and God will wipe away every tear from their eyes. (Rev. 7:16–17)*

Discussion Questions

1. Have you considered the ways Jesus is the glory of God revealed to us? What are some ways Jesus manifests God's glory?

2. Have you thought about what it means that you will share in God's glory—in his divine nature? When you think on it, does it cause praise and thankfulness to God to well up inside or an inner self-exaltation? Why?

3. What would it look like for you to receive the bread of God as a child? How would that bring him glory and bring you joy?

HOLIDAY CHOCOLATE BABKA

This is an overnight recipe.[38] I tend to make this most often around Thanksgiving and Christmas, because these are very special loaves of the most glorious bread. Spread some butter on a toasted slice alongside a cup of coffee, and you've got dessert or breakfast!

DOUGH:

4¼ cups (530 grams) all-purpose flour

½ cup (100 grams) granulated sugar

2 teaspoons (6 or 7 grams) instant yeast

grated zest of half an orange

3 eggs

½ cup (118 grams) water

¾ (4 or 5 grams) teaspoon salt

⅔ cup (151 grams) unsalted butter room temperature

CHOCOLATE FILLING:

¾ cup (120 grams) semisweet or dark chocolate chips

½ cup (113 grams) unsalted butter

THE DAY BEFORE BAKING:

Whisk the flour, sugar, yeast, and zest in the large bowl of a stand mixer.

Switch to the dough hook and add eggs and 1/2 cup water. Mix with the dough hook until it comes together to form a mass (this should take a couple minutes). Add a little more water if it's not coming together.

Add the butter, one tablespoon at a time, mixing on low, until it's incorporated. Add the salt.

Mix for 10 minutes on medium. After 10 minutes, the dough should be smooth (scrape the bowl down if needed). If the dough is too sticky or wet, you can add a little flour.

Transfer the dough to a clean bowl, cover with plastic wrap, and put in the fridge overnight.

ON BAKING DAY:

In a small saucepan, melt the butter and chocolate together. Stir in the powdered sugar, cocoa, and cinnamon. The mixture should be a pourable paste (if it's on the thinner side, don't worry; it will be fine).

Line two 9x4-inch loaf pans with parchment paper (cut long rectangular strips that are 4 inches wide and about 15 inches long, which will make it easy to lift the loaves out of the pans after baking).

Line one baking sheet with parchment paper.

recipe and ingredients list continued on page 179

½ cup (50 grams) powdered sugar

⅓ cup (35 grams) cocoa powder

¼ teaspoon (1 or 2 grams) cinnamon

SYRUP:

⅓ cup (79 grams) water

6 tablespoons (75 grams) sugar

makes two loaves

Take the dough out of the fridge, turn it out on a floured counter, and divide it into two equal pieces. Put one piece back in the fridge.

Roll out the dough on the counter to a 10-inch width (horizontally) and 12-inch length.

Pour half of the chocolate mixture on the dough, spreading it evenly with a spatula, leaving a 1/2-inch border all around.

Roll up the dough so that it looks like a log. You can seal the end by dabbing a little water on the dough to make it stick.

Transfer the log to the lined baking sheet.

Repeat steps 5–8 with the second piece of dough.

Cover the two logs with plastic wrap and put them in the freezer for 10–20 minutes.

Remove the logs from the freezer. Cut the logs in half lengthwise, placing each half with the chocolate side up next to its other half. Pinch the top ends of the two pieces together, then lift one side over the other (keeping the chocolate side up the whole time) until the two pieces form a twisted loaf. Pinch the bottom ends together. (If the log is too long, you can trim off either side to make it neater.

Transfer the twisted loaf to the loaf pan. Repeat with the second loaf.

Cover both loaves with a tea towel or plastic wrap. Let them rise on the counter for 1 to 1½ hours.

Preheat the oven to 375 degrees. Bake for 30 minutes. A knife should come out of the middle clean (except for chocolate on it).

Make the syrup while the loaves are baking. Simmer the water and sugar in a saucepan for about 1 minute.

Brush the syrup on the loaves right when they come out of the oven. Let the loaves cool for 15–30 minutes.

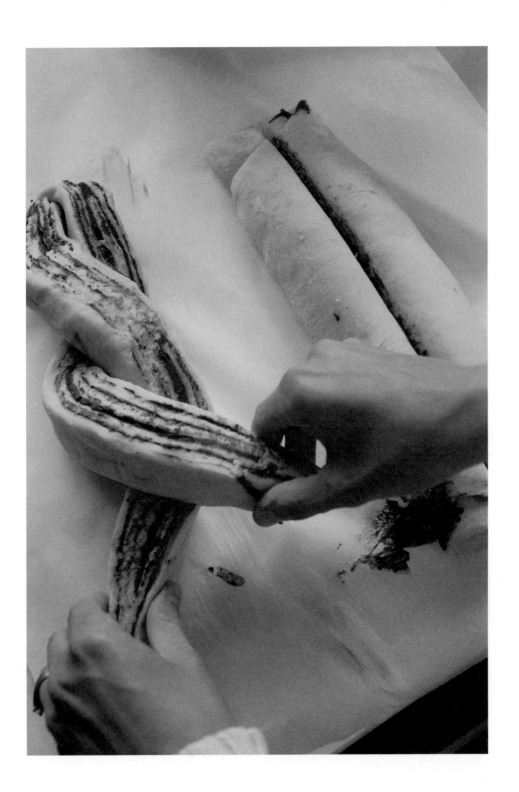

ACKNOWLEDGMENTS

Love one another with brotherly affection. Outdo one another in showing honor.

ROMANS 12:10

I love that Scripture tells us to honor one another. I love that it has categories for particular honor due to particular people. Honoring others is one of the happiest duties of a Christian. It is pure delight.

First, I honor those of you who have read all the way to these last paragraphs. Books need readers. I don't take that for granted in a day and age in which most people prefer bite-sized thoughts and bumper-sticker platitudes. I honor your commitment to engage with someone else's thoughts and words—to consider them, to immerse yourself in them, and to think critically about them. I pray it has been well-spent time.

I honor my mom, Bea, and my eldest daughter, Eliza, for helping take care of things so I could have weekly uninterrupted time during the two months this manuscript was written. Their service was always cheerful and breezy no matter what it was they were doing, and it made my heart glad and at ease.

I honor my three daughters Eliza, Elianna, and Evangeline, who tried out several recipes for me, baking in our kitchen without supervision, ensuring for the readers that my success with the recipes wasn't some sort of fluke. I also give thanks for all the happy eaters under my roof who make baking a joy, from regulars to guests, from family to those being folded in as family.

I honor the many sisters who prayed for me, for the content of this book, and for those of you who are reading it. Only the Lord truly knows what their prayers have afforded all of us. I am especially grateful to Laura Wifler and Emily Jensen for their eager prodding that I would get going on it, accompanied by their prayers. I honor the folks at Crossway who were willing to take a chance on this niche-genre book, and the talented team there that has worked with diligence, excellence, and joy to bring it into being. I honor the gospel partnership God has given us.

I honor my many editors and revisors for their thoughtful, probing, and relentlessly biblical feedback: Tom Dodds, Daniel and Jessica Souza, Kevin DeYoung, Aylin Merck, Emily Jensen, and Andy and Jenni Naselli. I am particularly thankful for the opportunity to trace the theme of bread through the Scriptures in Dr. Naselli's biblical theology class. The feedback from Dr. Naselli and fellow students was valuable and encouraging. The paper on bread that I wrote for that class was the instigation for the book proposal for *Bread of Life*, which the Lord gave me wind to write in the midst of school.

I honor my husband, Tom. Not only did he provide helpful feedback on the manuscript; he encouraged and strengthened me along the way. He is a faithful leader. It has been one of the biggest blessings of my life to follow him. He is a potent pointer to Jesus in the way he provides for us both physically and spiritually. This book certainly wouldn't exist without him.

Last, I honor the one who deserves all honor, God in three persons: Father, Son, and Spirit, blessed over all. This is all for you, Lord. Do with it whatever you will.

RECOMMENDED RESOURCES

Piper, John. "Look at the Book." *Desiring God* website. Accessed November 19, 2020. https://www.desiringgod.org/labs.

A video resource in which pastor John Piper slowly and carefully walks through a Bible passage, using a digital pen to write on the Bible text, teaching and explaining as he goes.

"To the Word: Bible Reading Challenge." Christ Church, Moscow, ID. Accessed November 19, 2020. https://biblereading.christkirk.com.

A Bible reading plan with the goal of getting women to read through the Bible regularly and consistently alongside other women. It includes #Keepthefeast, which is the plan for the school year and #Samepagesummer, which is the plan for the summer. These plans are available as a free printable or on the YouVersion Bible app. You can also join a Facebook group filled with more than ten thousand other women reading this plan.

"Memorize Scripture to Fight the Fight of Faith." *Truth:78* website. Accessed November 19, 2020. https://www.truth78.org/fighter-verses.

The "Fighter Verses" Scripture memory plan exists to help you memorize God's word. The Fighter Verses app has many wonderful tools to help you get started, including songs to help you memorize the verses.

NOTES

[1] You can find a kitchen scale fairly inexpensively online. To use one, put an empty bowl on the scale, "tare" the scale (*tare* means to set the scale to zero), then put flour or water or whatever is called for into the bowl until it reaches the desired amount of grams. To add another ingredient, tare the scale again and continue.

[2] For a book that very helpfully deals with four types of food-related sins, see Tilly Dillehay's *Broken Bread: How to Stop Using Food and Fear to Fill Spiritual Hunger* (Eugene, OR: Harvest, 2020).

[3] "The word of God is living and active, sharper than any two-edged sword, piercing to the division of soul and of spirit, of joints and of marrow, and discerning the thoughts and intentions of the heart" (Heb. 4:12). "Take the helmet of salvation, and the sword of the Spirit, which is the word of God" (Eph. 6:17).

[4] Joe Rigney, *Lewis on the Christian Life: Becoming Truly Human in the Presence of God*, Theologians on the Christian Life (Wheaton, IL: Crossway, 2018), 25. Joe has a wonderful meditation on this sentence of Lewis's in the beginning of this book, emphasizing each word and drawing out the implications. The first four sentences of this paragraph are a shameless condensing of his more sustained and helpful thought.

[5] C. S. Lewis, *Letters to Malcolm: Chiefly on Prayer*, 1st. ed. (New York: HarperCollins, 1964), 88.

[6] Adapted from "No-Knead Crusty Bread," *Simply So Good* website, September 19, 2018, https://www.simplysogood.com/wprm_print/12953. Variations of this recipe can be found high and low on the Internet! The no-knead approach originated with Jim Lahey in 2007.

[7] Elisabeth Elliot, *Discipline: The Glad Surrender* (Grand Rapids, MI: Revell, 2006), 10.

[8] Adapted from Alexandra Stafford's version of peasant bread. I've tried lots of focaccia recipes, and this one just always works. Plus it's completely no fuss. "My Mother's Peasant Bread: The Best, Easiest Bread You Will Ever Make," *Alexandra's Kitchen* website, November 7, 2012, https://alexandracooks.com/2012/11/07/my-mothers-peasant-bread-the-best-easiest-bread-you-will-ever-make/.

[9] My thinking on this was mainly aided by Sinclair Ferguson in his book *The Whole Christ*. He talks about abstraction as the root of both legalism and licentiousness. I commend the book to you. Sinclair B. Ferguson, *The Whole Christ: Legalism, Antino-*

mianism, and Gospel Assurance (Wheaton, IL: Crossway, 2016).

[10] Derek Kidner, *Genesis* (Downers Grove, IL: IVP Academic, 2019), 73.

[11] Kidner, *Genesis*, 73. See also Ligon Duncan, "The Whole in Our Holiness," presentation at Together for the Gospel, Louisville, KY, April 11–13, 2018, https://t4g.org/resources/ligon-duncan/the-whole-in-our-holiness/. Part of Duncan's talk was inspired by Kidner's *Genesis* commentary.

[12] Adapted from "Naan Bread," *Rasa Malaysia* website, accessed November 12, 2020, https://rasamalaysia.com/naan/#mv-creation-11.

[13] Τί ἐστιν τοῦτο is the Greek phrase in the Septuagint translated as "What is it?" and in the Greek New Testament as "What is this?" In the first case it refers to manna; in the second case, it refers to Jesus's teaching.

[14] Adapted from "Soft Cheese Bread," in Peter Reinhart, *Peter Reinhart's Artisan Breads Every Day: Fast and Easy Recipes for World-Class Breads*, 1st ed. (Berkeley, CA: Ten Speed Press, 2009), 118.

[15] Matthew Henry, *The Quest for Meekness and Quietness of Spirit* (Eugene, OR: Wipf & Stock, 2007), 18.

[16] Henry, *Quest for Meekness*, 18.

[17] Henry, *Quest for Meekness*, 19.

[18] Henry, *Quest for Meekness*, 19.

[19] Adapted from "Tartine's Country Bread" by Chad Robertson. His method and recipe are the gold standards for sourdough bread. "Tartine's Country Bread," *New York Times* website, accessed July 24, 2020, https://cooking.nytimes.com/recipes/1016277-tartines-country-bread.

[20] This is the first of many video tutorials on sourdough bread that you can find on my IGTV account (@abigail__dodds), or at my website: "Sourdough," *Abigail Dodds* website, accessed January 5, 2021, https://hopeandstay.com/hope-and-stay/sourdough/.

[21] Samuel Rutherford and Ellen S. Lister, *The Loveliness of Christ: Extracts from the Letters of Samuel Rutherford* (Carlisle, PA: Banner of Truth, 2007).

[22] Adapted from Mark Bittman, "Popovers," *New York Times* website, accessed July 24, 2020, https://cooking.nytimes.com/recipes/1012941-popovers.

[23] David W. Wead, "Bread of the Presence," *Baker Encyclopedia of the Bible* (Grand Rapids, MI: Baker, 1988), 379.

[24] Wead, "Bread of the Presence," 379.

[25] Rigney, *Lewis on the Christian Life*, 33.

[26] John M. Frame, *Systematic Theology: An Introduction to Christian Belief* (Phillipsburg, NJ: P&R, 2013), 1068.

[27] Adapted from "Farmhouse White Sandwich Bread," *Gather for Bread* website, June 15, 2015, https://gatherforbread.com/farmhouse-white-sandwich-bread/. This recipe doesn't really resemble the original anymore, as I've reduced it and changed some proportions.

[28] Elliot, *Discipline*, 31.

[29] Adapted from Chad Robertson's croissant recipe. His methods can seem fussy, but, boy, are they worth it. Chad Robertson, *Tartine Bread* (San Francisco: Chronicle, 2010), 160–70.

[30] This section was adapted from a preface to the Bible studies I've written for the women of my church beginning in 2016.

[31] Adapted from "The Best Biscuits Ever," Reinhart, *Peter Reinhart's Artisan Breads*, 175–80.

[32] From the Nicene Creed, https://en.wikipedia.org/wiki/Nicene_Creed.

[33] Nicene Creed; emphasis added.

[34] C. S. Lewis, *The Weight of Glory and Other Addresses*, rev. ed. (San Francisco: HarperSanFrancisco, 2001), 41.

[35] This is a riff on one of the most meaningful sentences I've ever read outside the Bible: "God is most glorified in us when we are most satisfied in him" by John Piper. If you'd like to explore this life-changing sentence more, I suggest you read John Piper, *Desiring God: Meditations of a Christian Hedonist* (Colorado Springs, CO: Multnomah, 1996), 10.

[36] Even those of you who are gluten free in your physical diet need never feel spiritually deprived! You have the Lord, your daily bread.

[37] I am not saying that Eve was not God's child or that she did not enter heaven when she died. I am simply commenting on what sin does to us.

[38] Adapted from Deb Perelman, "Better Chocolate Babka," *Smitten Kitchen* website, October 9, 2014, https://smittenkitchen.com/2014/10/better-chocolate-babka/. If you've never visited Smitten Kitchen online, you should remedy that. Deb Perelman is the cook behind the counter, the photos, and the delicious recipes.

GENERAL INDEX

SCRIPTURE INDEX

TECH FOR GOOD

THE FILM

SOURCES

PREFACE

1. https://www.margahoek.com/the-trillion-dollar-shift-book

Chapter 1: Tech for Good

1. https://www.weforum.org/focus/fourth-industrial-revolution
2. https://csis-website-prod.s3.amazonaws.com/s3fs-public/legacy_files/files/media/csis/pubs/071105_ageofconsequences.pdf
3. https://www.ipcc.ch/report/ar6/wg2/
4. https://news.un.org/en/story/2021/09/1098662
5. https://news.un.org/en/story/2021/09/1098662
6. https://seedscientific.com/plastic-waste-statistics/
7. https://www.unep.org/interactive/beat-plastic-pollution/
8. https://www.economist.com/graphic-detail/2018/03/06/only-9-of-the-worlds-plastic-is-recycled
9. https://www.telesurenglish.net/news/Plastic-Dump-as-Large-as-France-Germany-Spain-Together-Study-20180325-0037.html
10. https://www.weforum.org/agenda/2020/08/atlantic-ocean-plastic-pollution-study/#:~:text=The%20researchers%20estimate%20that%20the%20Atlantic%27s%20total%20plastic,released%20into%20the%20Atlantic%20between%201950%20and%202015.
11. https://www.worldatlas.com/articles/countries-putting-the-most-plastic-waste-into-the-oceans.html
12. https://www.statista.com/statistics/1228043/plastic-waste-generation-per-capita-in-select-countries/
13. https://www.ncbi.nlm.nih.gov/pmc/articles/PMC7896824/
14. https://emf.thirdlight.com/link/faarmdpz93ds-5vmvdf/@/preview/1?o
15. https://www.plasticssoupfoundation.org/en/plastic-problem/bogus-solutions/recycling-myth/#:~:text=In%20reality%2C%20only%209%25%20of%20all%20plastic%20in,or%20'virgin'%20plastic.%20Alliance%20to%20End%20Plastic%20Waste
16. https://covid19.who.int/table
17. https://www.apmresearchlab.org/covid/deaths-by-race
18. https://www.dni.gov/files/documents/Global%20Trends_2025%20Global%20Governance.pdf
19. https://www.thelancet.com/journals/lancet/article/PIIS0140-6736(20)30677-2/fulltext
20. https://www.unglobalcompact.org/sdgs/about
21. https://www.margahoek.com/the-trillion-dollar-shift-book/
22. https://sdgs.un.org/goals
23. https://unstats.un.org/sdgs/report/2021/investing-in-data-to-save-lives-and-build-back-better/
24. https://documents1.worldbank.org/curated/en/440191616164007723/pdf/Statistical-Performance-Indicators-and-Index-A-New-Tool-to-Measure-Country-Statistical-Capacity.pdf
25. https://www.nafham.com
26. https://www.wamda.com/2012/04/nafham-a-learning-management-platform-to-enhance-education-in-egypt
27. https://moocs4inclusion.org/index.php/catalogue/119-nafham
28. https://www.cairoscene.com/LifeStyle/Nafham-Education-for-All
29. https://www.egypttoday.com/Article/3/109951/Tyro-Nafham-acquisition-to-extend-user-base-tech-capabilities
30. https://www.wamda.com/2012/04/nafham-a-learning-management-platform-to-enhance-education-in-egypt
31. https://www.pwc.com/gx/en/news-room/press-releases/2019/ai-realise-gains-environment.html
32. https://www.bcg.com/publications/2018/tackling-1.6-billion-ton-food-loss-and-waste-crisis
33. https://www.who.int/news-room/fact-sheets/detail/malnutrition
34. https://www.fao.org/fileadmin/templates/wsfs/docs/expert_paper/How_to_Feed_the_World_in_2050.pdf
35. https://www.nrgene.com
36. https://www.phytech.com
37. https://www3.weforum.org/docs/WEF_Innovation_with_a_Purpose_VF-reduced.pdf
38. https://www.implicity.com
39. https://www.foreignaffairs.com/articles/world/2021-11-30/geopolitics-energy-green-upheaval?utm_source=Center+on+Global+Energy+olicy+Mailing+List&utm_campaign=d462abac2a-EMAIL_CAMPAIGN_2019_09_18_12_40_COPY_01&utm_medium=email&utm_term=0_0773077aac-d462abac2a-102060405
40. https://sdgs.un.org/goals/goal7
41. https://www.powergen-renewable-energy.com
42. https://www.lambda.energy/technology/
43. https://ngpartners.com/portfolio/
44. https://astute.global/2022-invest-in-future-supply-chain-technology/
45. https://www.provenance.org/tracking-tuna-on-the-blockchain#:~:text=Provenance%20focused%20deployment%20in%20two%20main%20supply%20chains%3A,in%20Ambon%20for%20production%20at%20a%20local%20cannery.
46. https://www.skuchain.com
47. https://www.wto.org/english/res_e/booksp_e/tradefinnace19_e.pdf
48. https://www.marketwatch.com/press-release/wood-recycling-market-exhibits-a-stunning-growth-potentials-by-2025-2021-10-18
49. https://www.actandsorb.com
50. https://www.wired.com/story/we-need-to-build-up-digital-trust-in-tech/
51. https://papers.ssrn.com/sol3/papers.cfm?abstract_id=2466040
52. https://medium.com/swlh/you-trust-the-algorithm-more-than-the-human-4760f7213a0a
53. https://www.freepressjournal.in/tech/83-of-indians-trust-ai-bots-over-people-to-manage-finances-study
54. https://wuga.org/post/trusting-algorithm-uga-research-shows-people-rely-more-algorithms-people-0#stream/0
55. https://www.freepressjournal.in/tech/man-vs-machine-people-trust-computers-more-than-humans-finds-a-study
56. https://www.edelman.com/research/2019-trust-tech-wavering-companies-must-act
57. https://www.edelman.com/research/2019-trust-tech-wavering-companies-must-act
58. https://www.allconnect.com/blog/consumer-trust-in-technology-fell-to-an-all-time-low-in-2021
59. https://www.wired.com/story/we-need-to-build-up-digital-trust-in-tech/
60. https://www.amazon.com/Tech-Life-Putting-trust-technology/dp/877192065X
61. https://www.globaljustice.org.uk/news/69-richest-100-entities-planet-are-corporations-not-governments-figures-show/

62. https://companiesmarketcap.com/largest-companies-by-revenue/
63. https://www.businessinsider.com/25-giant-companies-that-earn-more-than-entire-countries-2018-7#visa-made-more-in-2017-than-bosnias-gdp-4
64. https://www.routledge.com/The-Trillion-Dollar-Shift/Hoek/p/book/9780815364313
65. http://businesscommission.org/news/better-leadership-better-world
66. https://www.ansoffmatrix.com
67. Graphic subject to copyright, 2023, Marga Hoek
68. https://www.unilever.com
69. https://www.google.com
70. https://cloud.google.com/press-releases/2020/0922/unilever-to-reimagine-future-of-sustainable-sourcing
71. https://www.unilever.com/news/news-and-features/Feature-article/2020/how-google-will-help-end-deforestation-in-our-supply-chain.html
72. https://www.unilever.com/news/press-releases/2019/unilevers-purpose-led-brands-outperform.html#:~:text=In%202018%2C%20Unilever's%20Sustainable%20Living%20Brands%20grew%2069%25,Up%20%28toothpaste%29%2C%20Wheel%20%28laundry%29%2C%20Calve%20and%20Bango%20%28dressings%29%3B
73. https://hbr.org/2011/01/the-big-idea-creating-shared-value
74. https://www.dsm.com/corporate/news/news-archive/2018/30-18-dsm-tops-dow-jones-sustainability-world-index.html
75. https://www.interface.com/APAC/en-SEA/campaign/climate-take-back/Sustainability-A-Look-Back-en_SEA
76. https://www.interface.com/US/en-US/sustainability/our-mission.html
77. https://www.interface.com/US/en-US.html?r=1
78. https://www.interface.com/US/en-US/sustainability/our-mission.html
79. https://www.interface.com/US/en-US/sustainability/sustainability-overview.html
80. https://www3.weforum.org/docs/Unlocking_Technology_for_the_Global_Goals.pdf
81. https://theworldwecreate.net
82. https://www.grandviewresearch.com/industry-analysis/artificial-intelligence-ai-market
83. https://3dprintingindustry.com/news/3d-hubs-am-trends-report-reveals-3d-printing-grew-21-despite-covid-19-189087/
84. https://www.mordorintelligence.com/industry-reports/robotics-market
85. https://greencleanguide.com/how-robotics-is-revolutionizing-sustainability/
86. https://www.industryarc.com/Report/15380/advanced-materials-market.html
87. https://www.mordorintelligence.com/industry-reports/extended-reality-xr-market
88. https://ieeexplore.ieee.org/document/8699256
89. https://www.grandviewresearch.com/industry-analysis/global-commercial-drones-market#:~:text=The%20global%20commercial%20drone%20market%20size%20was%20valued,was%20recorded%20at%20689.4%20thousand%2-0units%20in%202020.
90. https://www.alliedmarketresearch.com/autonomous-vehicle-market#:~:text=The%20global%20autonomous%20vehicle%20market%20size%20is%20projected,a%20CAGR%20of%20 39.47%25%20from%202019%20to%202026.
91. https://www.forbes.com/sites/bernardmarr/2020/07/17/5-ways-self-driving-cars-could-make-our-world-and-our-lives-better/?sh=3c5e838b42a3
92. https://www.cryptocurrencywire.com/crypto-companies/stronghold-digital-mining-inc/#:~:text=According%20to%20a%20market%20analysis%20report%20from%20Grand,market%20worth%20a%20whopping%20%24450%20bi-llion%20by%202028.
93. https://www.accenture.com/_acnmedia/pdf-68/accenture-808045-blockchainpov-rgb.pdf
94. https://www.feedough.com/what-is-space-tech/
95. https://analytics.dkv.global/spacetech/SpaceTech-Industry-2021-Report.pdf
96. https://unctad.org/system/files/official-document/ecn162020d3_en.pdf
97. https://www3.weforum.org/docs/Unlocking_Technology_for_the_Global_Goals.pdf
98. https://www.iotscot.com/#:~:text=These%20devices%20range%20from%20ordinary%20household%20objects%20to,to%20grow%20to%2022%20billion%20by%202025.%201
99. https://www.smartcultiva.com/hydroponic_sensing_devices_monitor_farm.html
100. https://www.startus-insights.com/innovators-guide/5-top-urban-farming-startups-impacting-smart-cities/
101. https://s3.amazonaws.com/sustainabledevelopment.report/2019/2019_sustainable_development_report.pdf
102. https://www.wipo.int/edocs/pubdocs/en/wipo_pub_gii_2019.pdf
103. https://www.itu.int/hub/2021/11/facts-and-figures-2021-2-9-billion-people-still-offline/
104. https://www.itu.int/hub/2021/11/facts-and-figures-2021-2-9-billion-people-still-offline/
105. https://www.sciencedirect.com/science/article/abs/pii/S0959652620307927
106. https://www.techtarget.com/whatis/definition/moonshot
107. https://www.techtarget.com/whatis/definition/moonshot
108. https://blogs.microsoft.com/blog/2020/01/16/microsoft-will-be-carbon-negative-by-2030/
109. https://x.company/careers-at-x/5254181002/
110. https://x.company
111. https://x.company/projects/loon/
112. https://blog.x.company/loon-draft-c3fcebc11f3f
113. https://blog.x.company/loons-final-flight-e9d699123a96

Chapter 2: AI and Data

1. https://searchenterpriseai.techtarget.com/feature/Agri-cutural-AI-yields-better-crops-through-data-analytics
2. https://www.fortunebusinessinsights.com/industry-reports/artificial-intelligence-market-100114
3. https://www.thebusinessresearchcompany.com/report/artificial-intelligence-market-global-report-2020-30-co-vid-19-growth-and-change
4. http://breakthrough.unglobalcompact.org/site/assets/files/1454/hhw-16-0017-d_c_artificial_intelligence.pdf
5. https://www.statista.com/statistics/607716/worldwide-artificial-ai-intelligence-market-revenues/
6. https://www.grandviewresearch.com/press-release/global-arti-ficial-intelligence-ai-market
7. http://breakthrough.unglobalcompact.org/site/assets/files/1454/hhw-16-0017-d_c_artificial_intelligence.pdf
8. https://www.accenture.com/gb-en/insights/strategy/green-behind-cloud?c=acn_glb_greenbehindthecgoog-le_11599320&n=psgs_1020
9. https://www.mordorintelligence.com/industry-reports/smart-building-market#:~:text=The%20smart%20building%20market%20was%20valued%20at%20USD,infrastructure%20projects%20are%20driving%20the%20market%27s%20growth%20positively.
10. https://www.accenture.com/us-en/insights/artificial-intelligen-ce-summary-index
11. https://www.fortunebusinessinsights.com/industry-reports/artificial-intelligence-market-100114

12. https://www.fortunebusinessinsights.com/industry-reports/artificial-intelligence-market-100114

13. https://www.fortunebusinessinsights.com/industry-reports/artificial-intelligence-market-100114

14. https://builtin.com/artificial-intelligence/ai-trading-stock-market-tech

15. https://www.lab49.com

16. https://www.lab49.com/insights/using-ai-to-drive-sustainable-investment/

17. https://www.lab49.com/insights/using-ai-to-drive-sustainable-investment/

18. https://databricks.com/blog/2020/07/10/a-data-driven-approach-to-environmental-social-and-governance.html

19. https://www.nvidia.com/en-us/

20. https://developer.nvidia.com/blog/nuance-accelerates-conversational-ai-training-by-50/

21. https://www.capgemini.com/research/climate-ai/

22. https://www.mckinsey.com/featured-insights/artificial-intelligence/notes-from-the-ai-frontier-applications-and-value-of-deep-learning

23. https://www.mckinsey.com/featured-insights/artificial-intelligence/notes-from-the-ai-frontier-applications-and-value-of-deep-learning

24. https://www.mckinsey.com/featured-insights/artificial-intelligence/notes-from-the-ai-frontier-applications-and-value-of-deep-learning

25. https://www.globenewswire.com/news-release/2023/02/16/2609849/0/en/Global-Artificial-Intelligence-AI-Market-to-Generate-USD-1847-58-Billion-by-2030-Outlines-a-New-Report-by-Next-Move-Strategy-Consulting.html#:~:text=New%20York%2C%20Feb.,32.9%25%20from%202022%20to%202030.

26. https://www.statista.com/statistics/1365145/artificial-intelligence-market-size/#:~:text=The%20market%20for%20artificial%20intelligence,nearly%20two%20trillion%20U.S.%20dollars

27. https://www.grandviewresearch.com/industry-analysis/advanced-analytics-market

28. https://www.ecomena.org/artificial-intelligence-environmental-sustainability/

29. https://www.mckinsey.com/featured-insights/artificial-intelligence/applying-artificial-intelligence-for-social-good#

30. https://ssir.org/articles/entry/artificial_intelligence_as_a_force_for_good#

31. https://earth.org/data_visualization/ai-can-it-help-achieve-environmental-sustainable/

32. https://www.datacenterknowledge.com/machine-learning/ai-data-center-management-what-it-means-staffing-and-processes?utm_source=riq&utm_campaign=2510&utm_term=abhinandanghosh

33. https://www.forbes.com/sites/bernardmarr/2020/02/10/8-powerful-examples-of-ai-for-good/#3243c65dd18a

34. https://www.accenture.com/us-en/insights/artificial-intelligence/ai-investments

35. https://www.microsoft.com/en-us/?ql=4

36. https://www.google.com

37. https://www.microsoft.com/en-us/ai/ai-for-earth

38. https://ai.google/social-good

39. https://www.cnbc.com/2018/02/01/google-ceo-sundar-pichai-ai-is-more-important-than-fire-electricity.html

40. https://techhq.com/2020/09/can-tech-giants-bring-the-ai-fight-to-climate-change/

41. https://economictimes.indiatimes.com/news/economy/policy/microsoft-and-niti-aayog-partner-to-deploy-ai-solution/articleshow/66184093.cms?from=mdr

42. https://www.realclearscience.com/articles/2018/06/30/china_is_spearheading_the_future_of_agriculture.html

43. https://about.google/stories/clean-air-for-kampala/

44. https://www.information-age.com/how-retailers-can-use-ai-drive-sustainability-profits-simultaneously-123491887/

45. https://www.pwc.com/gx/en/issues/analytics/assets/pwc-ai-analysis-sizing-the-prize-report.pdf

46. https://www.aspentech.com/en/resources/blog/artificial-intelligence-and-sustainability-safer-greener-and-smarter-operations

47. https://www.technologyreview.com/2018/06/27/141803/ai-as-a-force-for-good/

48. https://arju.org/2019/08/30/communities-control-artificial-intelligence/

49. https://data-for-good.com

50. https://bigdatablock.com/big-data-just-how-big-is-it/

51. http://blog.globalforestwatch.org/data/how-artificial-intelligence-helped-us-predict-forest-loss-in-the-democratic-republic-of-the-congo.html

52. https://www.blog.google/topics/machine-learning/fight-against-illegal-deforestation-tensorflow/

53. https://ssir.org/articles/entry/artificial_intelligence_as_a_force_for_good#

54. https://ai-for-sdgs.academy/ai4sdgs-cooperation-network

55. https://www.nature.com/articles/s41467-019-14108-y

56. https://okra.ai

57. https://www.mckinsey.com/~/media/mckinsey/featured%20insights/artificial%20intelligence/applying%20artificial%20intelligence%20for%20social%20good/mgi-applying-ai-for-social-good-discussion-paper-dec-2018.ashx

58. https://www.technocracy.news/ai-accelerating-uns-sustainable-development-goals-sdgs/#:~:text=SDG%2012%3A%20Responsible%20consumption%20and%20production%20AI%20is,infused%20with%20AI%20pre%C2%ADdicts%20climate-related%20problems%20and%20disasters.

59. https://ai4good.org/blog/harnessing-ai-for-renewable-energy-access-in-africa/

60. https://omdena.com/projects/ai-renewable-energy/?mc_cid=cba6e8e732&mc_eid=a03020ad85

61. https://ai4good.org/ai-for-sdgs/goal-7-affordable-clean-energy/

62. https://ai.google/about/

63. https://www.isize.co

64. https://www.technologyreview.com/2018/06/27/141803/ai-as-a-force-for-good/

65. https://ai4good.org/ai-for-sdgs/goal-12-responsible-consumption-production/

66. https://www.wasteless.com

67. https://venturebeat.com/2021/01/04/amp-robotics-raises-55-million-for-ai-that-picks-and-sorts-recyclables/

68. https://www.capgemini.com/research/climate-ai/

69. https://techcrunch.com/2021/06/03/one-concern-sompo/

70. https://www.forbes.com/sites/robtoews/2021/06/20/these-are-the-startups-applying-ai-to-tackle-climate-change/?sh=6c0500217b26

71. https://us.nttdata.com/en/engage/ai-study-ai-accelerated?mkwid=s_dc&pcrid=&pkw=%2Bbusiness%20%2Bartificial%20%2Bintelligence&pmt=p&msclkid=0e96f48d4571139bb-ba495b29baf2d91&utm_source=bing&utm_medium=cpc&utm_campaign=US_GS_Services_Data_AI_and_Automation_BMM&utm_term=%2Bbusiness%20%2Bartificial%20%2Bintelligence&utm_content=Artificial%20Intelligence

72. https://www.forbes.com/sites/cognitiveworld/2019/07/10/how-artificial-intelligence-is-transforming-business-models/?sh=2c9fd6132648

73. https://www.avanade.com/en-us

74. https://www.avanade.com/en/blogs/avanade-insights/responsible-business/msft-cloud-sustainability-services

75. https://siliconangle.com/2021/07/15/the-new-approach-to-integrations-automated-closed-loop-and-multi-style-think2021/

76. https://transvoyant.com

77. https://www.youtube.com/watch?v=ErY2YjrLgGU
78. https://dukespace.lib.duke.edu/dspace/bitstream/handle/10161/12742/DiMasi-Grabowski-Hansen-RnD-JHE-2016.pdf;sequence=1
79. https://bekryl.com/industry-trends/ai-artificial-intelligence-in-drug-discovery-market-size-analysis
80. https://www.mckinsey.com/~/media/mckinsey/featured%20insights/artificial%20intelligence/applying%20artificial%20intelligence%20for%20social%20good/mgi-applying-ai-for-social-good-discussion-paper-dec-2018.pdf
81. https://searchenterpriseai.techtarget.com/feature/Agricultural-AI-yields-better-crops-through-data-analytics
82. https://www.corti.ai
83. https://www.theverge.com/2018/4/25/17278994/ai-cardiac-arrest-corti-emergency-call-response
84. https://www.cnet.com/paid-content/features/ai-enables-the-future-of-farming/
85. https://www.microsoft.com/en-us/research/project/farmbeats-iot-agriculture/
86. https://www.futurefarming.com/Smart-farmers/Articles/2018/9/Microsoft-Great-potential-for-AI-in-agriculture-331961E/
87. https://www.forbes.com/sites/bernardmarr/2020/02/10/8-powerful-examples-of-ai-for-good/#7e93b085d18a
88. https://sinews.siam.org/Details-Page/farmbeats-improving-farm-productivity-using-data-driven-agriculture
89. https://www.microsoft.com/en-us/research/project/farmbeats-iot-agriculture/
90. https://www.gatesnotes.com/Development/FarmBeats
91. https://emerj.com/ai-sector-overviews/ai-crime-prevention-5-current-applications/
92. https://emerj.com/ai-sector-overviews/ai-crime-prevention-5-current-applications/#:~:text=Last%20year%20Hikvision%2C%20a%20Chinese%20company%20which%20is,to%20run%20deep%20neural%20networks%20right%20on%20board.
93. https://www.hikvision.com/en/newsroom/latest-news/2021/hikvision-announces-2021-first-half-year-financial-results/
94. https://www.mordorintelligence.com/industry-reports/smart-building-market
95. https://www.nrdc.org/experts/jake-schmidt/deforestation-costs-worldwow-big
96. https://www.mckinsey.com/~/media/mckinsey/featured%20insights/artificial%20intelligence/applying%20artificial%20intelligence%20for%20social%20good/mgi-applying-ai-for-social-good-discussion-paper-dec-2018.pdf
97. https://www.forbes.com/sites/bernardmarr/2020/02/10/8-powerful-examples-of-ai-for-good/#7e93b085d18a
98. http://squirrelai.com
99. https://www.quill.org
100. https://www.capgemini.com
101. https://www.capgemini.com/news/inside-stories/mojave-desert/?utm_source=aez&utm_medium=social&utm_content=none_advocacy_web-preview_landingpage_mojave&utm_campaign=corporate_brand
102. https://defenders.org/sites/default/files/publications/economic_oasis.pdf
103. https://www.nps.gov/moja/learn/news/tourism-to-mojave-national-preserve-creates-nearly-43-million-in-economic-benefits-in-2015.htm
104. https://www.techcircle.in/2022/01/19/capgemini-builds-ai-solution-to-help-conserve-mojave-desert
105. https://ai4good.org/what-we-do/sdg-launchpad/
106. https://www.getsmarter.com/products/mit-sloan-artificial-intelligence-implications-for-business-strategy-online-program?utm_campaign=MIT_AI_KIT1_INT&utm_medium=campaign&utm_source=email
107. https://executive.mit.edu/on/demandware.static/-/Sites-master-catalog-msee/default/dwaa8ddbd9/brochures/ai-online-program-brochure.pdf
108. https://www.cognii.com
109. https://www.netexlearning.com/en/e-learning-for-companies/
110. https://www.netexlearning.com/en/case-studies/valencia-international-university/
111. https://elexsys.com/
112. https://think-tank-talk.org/2019/12/04/how-artificial-intelligence-can-make-more-of-energy/
113. https://www.nnergix.com/software?lang=en
114. https://www.indiatoday.in/india/story/why-india-does-not-have-enough-water-to-drink-1557669-2019-06-28
115. https://www.epa.gov/watersense/statistics-and-facts
116. https://www.analyticsinsight.net/the-promise-of-artificial-intelligence-in-water-management/#:~:text=AI%20can%20make%20the%20process%20of%20water%20management,and%20to%20get%20the%20status%20of%20water%20resources.
117. https://www.mckinsey.com/featured-insights/future-of-work/jobs-lost-jobs-gained-what-the-future-of-work-will-mean-for-jobs-skills-and-wages
118. https://www.simplilearn.com/advantages-and-disadvantages-of-artificial-intelligence-article#:~:text=A%20big%20disadvantage%20of%20AI%20is%20that%20it,data%20and%20facts%20already%20provided%20to%20the%20bot.

Chapter 3: 3D Printing

1. https://www.noaa.gov/education/resource-collections/marine-life/coral-reef-ecosystems#:~:text=Coral%20reefs%20protect%20coastlines%20from%20storms%20and%20erosion%2C,depend%20on%20reefs%20for%20food%2C%20income%2C%20and%20protection.
2. https://www.nature.com/scitable/blog/saltwater-science/why_are_coral_reefs_important/
3. https://www.manilatimes.net/2019/12/22/opinion/analysis/plastic-the-largest-predator-in-our-oceans/666425/
4. https://3dprint.com/209832/xtreee-seaboost-coral-reef/
5. http://www.secore.org/site/home.html
6. https://www.3printr.com/3d-printed-nanosculptures-jonty-hurwitz-1422352/
7. https://composites.umaine.edu
8. https://www.statista.com/topics/1969/additive-manufacturing-and-3d-printing/
9. https://fitmyfoot.com/pages/science
10. https://3dprintingindustry.com/news/cornell-hp-and-nasa-successfully-test-3d-modeling-software-aboard-iss-203494/
11. https://www.launcherspace.com
12. https://www.velo3d.com
13. https://louisville.edu/amist/
14. https://www.3dhubs.com/knowledge-base/aerospace-3d-printing-applications/
15. https://reprap.org/wiki/RepRap
16. https://www.fastcompany.com/90497468/the-3d-printing-revolution-is-finally-here
17. https://www.saveur.com/3d-printers-pasta-barilla/
18. https://www.bcn3d.com/the-history-of-3d-printing-when-was-3d-printing-invented/
19. https://3dprintingindustry.com/news/3d-hubs-am-trends-report-reveals-3d-printing-grew-21-despite-covid-19-189087/
20. https://3dprintingindustry.com/news/3d-hubs-am-trends-report-reveals-3d-printing-grew-21-despite-covid-19-189087/
21. https://mordorintelligence.com/industry-reports/3d-printing-market
22. https://paulmampillyguru.com/america-2-0/3d-printing-companies/?utm_source=BPD-Newsletter&utm_medium=Email&utm_campaign=Daily-Article-Traffic

23. https://www.ibtimes.com/how-3d-printing-can-impact-climate-change-business-decade-2997574
24. https://amfg.ai/2019/05/29/expert-interview-zachary-murphree-velo3d/
25. https://3dprintingindustry.com/news/system-sales-boom-drives-stratasys-return-to-growth-in-q1-2021-189638/
26. https://www.gartner.com/en/information-technology/glossary/hype-cycle
27. https://3dprintingindustry.com/news/3d-hubs-am-trends-report-reveals-3d-printing-grew-21-despite-covid-19-189087/
28. https://www.grandviewresearch.com/industry-analysis/3d-printing-industry-analysis
29. https://3dprintingindustry.com/news/3d-hubs-am-trends-report-reveals-3d-printing-grew-21-despite-covid-19-189087/
30. https://www.hubs.com/get/trends/
31. https://www.marketsandmarkets.com/Market-Reports/3d-printing-medical-devices-market-90799911.html
32. https://mordorintelligence.com/industry-reports/3d-printing-market
33. https://www.prnewswire.com/news-releases/additive-manufacturing-market-size-to-grow-at-a-cagr-of-21-75--valuates-reports-301604973.html
34. https://www.marketsandmarkets.com/Market-Reports/3d-printing-medical-devices-market-90799911.html
35. https://www.energy.gov/sites/default/files/2019/07/f64/2019-OTT-Additive-Manufacturing-Spotlight_0.pdf
36. https://www.energy.gov/sites/default/files/2019/07/f64/2019-OTT-Additive-Manufacturing-Spotlight_0.pdf
37. https://www.ted.com/talks/avi_reichental_what_s_next_in_3d_printing?language=en#t-87021
38. https://www.whitehouse.gov/cea/written-materials/2022/05/09/using-additive-manufacturing-to-improve-supply-chain-resilience-and-bolster-small-and-mid-size-firms/
39. https://www.astroa.org/amforward
40. https://www.fictiv.com/articles/6-industries-being-transformed-by-3d-printing
41. https://www.siemens.com/global/en.html
42. https://www.stratasys.com/explore/case-study/siemens-rrx
43. https://www.tctmagazine.com/additive-manufacturing-3d-printing-news/siemens-mobility-digital-rail-maintenance-3d-print-spare-parts/
44. https://www.stratasys.com/explore/case-study/siemens-supply-chain
45. https://www.fastcompany.com/40538464/this-house-can-be-3d-printed-for-4000
46. https://genecis.co/
47. https://www.novameat.com
48. https://organovo.com
49. https://markforged.com/industries/medical
50. https://3dprintingindustry.com/news/mit-3d-printed-cups-deliver-multiple-vaccines-single-shot-121348/#google_vignette
51. https://www.pnas.org/content/118/39/e2102595118
52. https://scitechdaily.com/3d-printed-vaccine-patch-offers-vaccination-without-a-shot-outperforms-needle-jab-in-boosting-immunity/
53. https://blueskypit.com/2021/06/21/texas-manufacturer-joins-neighborhood-91/
54. https://3dprintingindustry.com/news/analyzing-the-economic-impact-of-the-neighborhood-91-additive-manufacturing-hub-at-pittsburgh-international-airport-167286/
55. https://neighborhood91.com
56. https://www.lm-innovations.com/en-gb/plants/alpha-140/
57. https://www.3dprintingmedia.network/new-raw-plastic-waste-3d-furniture/
58. https://www.winsun3dbuilders.com
59. https://goexplorer.org/3d-printed-structures-save-time/
60. https://3drific.com/can-i-make-money-with-a-3d-printer-and-how/
61. https://markets.businessinsider.com/news/stocks/shapeways-expands-traditional-manufacturing-offerings-1030426002
62. https://www.3dquickprinting.com/rapid-prototyping/6-advantages-rapid-prototyping/#:~:text=Rapid%20prototyping%20comes%20with%20a%20myriad%20of%20advantages.,create%20real%20scale%20models%20for%20inspection%20and%20analysis.
63. https://www.mscdirect.com/betterMRO/msc-generate-pdf/11201
64. https://www.raise3d.com/why-raise3d/
65. https://en.tctasia.cn/asia_abouttctasia.shtml
66. https://www.basf.com/global/en/who-we-are/organization/group-companies/BASF_New-Business-GmbH/news/press-releases/2021/210526_forward-am-raise3d.html#:~:text=BASF%203D%20Printing%20Solutions%20GmbH%2C%20headquartered%20in%20Heidelberg%2C,and%20services%20in%20the%20field%20of%203D%20printing.
67. https://www.raise3d.com/news/raise3d-launches-metalfuse-a-3d-printing-full-in-house-solution-using-ultrafuse-metal-filaments-from-basf-forward-am-which-allows-small-batch-production-of-metal-parts-with-full-design-freed/
68. https://www.raise3d.com/news/raise3d-announces-15-8-million-in-series-c-funding/
69. https://www.makerbot.com/stories/engineering/advantages-of-3d-printing/
70. https://www.makerbot.com/stories/design/3d-printing-materials/
71. https://amfg.ai/2018/04/30/professor-ian-campbell-loughborough-university/
72. https://www.bcn3d.com
73. https://www.bcn3d.com/3d-printing-revolutionizes-product-design-at-camper/
74. https://www.3dprintingmedia.network/3d-printing-camper-shoe-design/
75. https://3dprint.com/261120/camper-spanish-footwear-designed-on-3d-printers-island-mallorca/
76. https://newsroom.accenture.com/news/the-circular-economy-could-unlock-4-5-trillion-of-economic-growth-finds-new-book-by-accenture.htm
77. https://www.mckinsey.com/business-functions/sustainability/our-insights/growth-within-a-circular-economy-vision-for-a-competitive-europe
78. https://sustainabilitydictionary.com/2005/12/03/cradle-to-cradle/
79. https://www2.deloitte.com/us/en/insights/focus/3d-opportunity/additive-manufacturing-3d-opportunity-in-tooling.html
80. https://www.sciencedirect.com/science/article/abs/pii/S0301421514004868
81. https://redetec.com/
82. https://www.filabot.com/products/filabot-reclaimer-1
83. https://www.3dnatives.com/en/protocycler-recycling-system-3d-printer-3d-prints-plastic-waste-151120185/
84. https://www.3ders.org/articles/20170224-protocycler-the-desktop-filament-maker-aiming-to-make-3d-printing-more-sustainable.html
85. https://medtech3d.co.za
86. https://axial3d.com
87. https://www.3dprintingmedia.network/medtech3d-axial3d-3d-printing-south-african-hospitals/
88. https://axial3d.com/latest/axial3d-partners-with-medtech3d-to-bring-3d-printing-to-hospitals-in-south-africa
89. https://www.epa.gov/facts-and-figures-about-materials-waste-and-recycling/plastics-material-specific-data#:~:text=While%20overall%20the%20amount%20of,plastic%20containers%20is%20more%20significant.
90. http://www3.weforum.org/docs/WEF_The_New_Plastics_Economy.pdf

91. https://3devo.com
92. https://all3dp.com/2/the-3d-printer-filament-recycler-s-guide/
93. https://news.un.org/en/story/2013/09/448652
94. https://news.un.org/en/story/2013/09/448652
95. https://www.Uprintingfood.com
96. https://www.verywellhealth.com/bioprinting-in-medicine-4691000
97. https://www.polarismarketresearch.com/industry-analysis/bone-grafts-substitutes-market
98. https://www.verywellhealth.com/skin-grafts-in-reconstructive-surgery-2710284
99. https://banyanhill.com/america-2-0-rx-double-stock-buy-3d-printed-bones/
100. https://luxurylaunches.com/other_stuff/a_3d_replica_of_your_fetus_serves_as_a_prenatal_memorabilia.php
101. https://www.huffpost.com/entry/3d-printer-inventions_n_4262091
102. https://www.3dsystems.com/healthcare
103. https://3dprint.com/248192/interview-with-tendai-pasipanodya-on-integrating-3d-printing-with-the-uns-sustainable-development-goals/
104. https://menafn.com/1102152730/Middle-East-and-Africa-3D-printing-in-healthcare-Market-SWOT-Analysis-Size-Share-Growth-Rate-Application-Types-Future-Demand-Business-Opportunity-Key-Indicators-and-Forecast-2030
105. https://www.businesswire.com/news/home/20190404005026/en/Global-Orthopedic-3D-Printing-Devices-Market-2019-2023
106. https://3dprint.com/242729/3d-printing-in-africa-kenya-3d-printing/
107. https://vc4a.com/ventures/micrive-infinite-limited/
108. https://www.businessdailyafrica.com/corporate/tech/3D-printing-venture-changed-surgery/4258474-5096532-r9xs39/index.html
109. https://www.framlab.com https://www.dezeen.com/2017/11/21/homed-famlab-parasitic-hexagonal-pods-new-york-homeless-shelters/
110. https://3dprintingindustry.com/news/interview-framlab-creatives-behind-3d-printed-homed-shelters-nyc-127311/
111. https://www.inexhibit.com/case-studies/homed-framlab-modular-housing-units-homeless-people-new-york-city/
112. https://www.3dprintingmedia.network/icon-new-story-create-4000-3d-printed-house-developing-world/
113. https://propertyregistry.com.au/how-long-does-it-take-to-build-a-house/#:~:text=If%20you%20decide%20to%20build,completed%20between%204%2D7%20months.
114. https://www.3dprintingmedia.network/homed-concept-framlab-explores-3d-printed-pods-address-nycs-homeless-issues/
115. https://www.wsj.com/articles/new-york-citys-spending-on-homeless-hits-3-2-billion-this-year-11558562997
116. https://ibo.nyc.ny.us/iboreports/adams-increases-funds-for-homeless-shelters-but-more-needed-for-shelters-and-other-programs-fopb-march-2022.pdf
117. https://www.iconbuild.com/updates/icon-delivers-series-of-3d-printed-homes-for-homeless
118. https://www.dwell.com/article/community-first-3d-printed-houses-icon-mobile-loaves-and-fishes-3f950815
119. https://www.iconbuild.com/faq
120. https://www.iconbuild.com/updates/icon-delivers-series-of-3d-printed-homes-for-homeless
121. https://weprinthomes.com
122. https://newstorycharity.org
123. https://www.weforum.org/agenda/2019/12/3d-printed-homes-neighborhood-tabasco-mexico
124. https://3dprintingindustry.com/news/icon-unveils-plans-for-improved-next-generation-vulcan-3d-printer-190706/
125. https://bisresearch.com
126. https://interestingengineering.com/3d-printing-will-change-the-way-you-eat-in-2020-and-beyond
127. https://www.nasa.gov/directorates/spacetech/home/feature_3d_food.html
128. https://www.channelnewsasia.com/news/cnainsider/how-3d-food-printing-can-help-the-elderly-nutrition-12470760
129. https://www.anrich3d.com/about
130. https://www.foodnavigator-asia.com/Article/2021/03/23/Mathematically-optimised-meals-Singapore-3D-food-printing-firm-ready-for-commercialisation-with-personalised-nutrition-technology
131. https://agrifoodinnovationevent.com/exhibitor/anrich3d-is-start-up-partner-of-agrifood-innovation-event/
132. https://doi.org/10.3920/978-90-8686-813-1_2
133. https://www.asme.org/topics-resources/content/solving-world-hunger-3dprinted-food
134. https://sffsymposium.engr.utexas.edu/Manuscripts/2011/2011-03-Baumers.pdf
135. https://3dinsider.com/3d-printers-for-sale/
136. https://3dinsider.com/3d-printing-filaments/
137. https://pubs.acs.org/doi/pdf/10.1021/acs.est.5b04983
138. https://www.rtds-group.com/services/projects/performance/?portfolioID=100
139. https://www.digitalfoodprocessing.com/en/digitalfoodprocessing/show/printing-meals-the-elderly-can-enjoy-again.htm

Chapter 4: Robotics

1.   https://www.autismspeaks.org/autism-statistics-asd
2.   https://embodied.com
3.   https://www.nytimes.com/2020/04/27/nyregion/coronavirus-homeschooling-parents.html
4.   https://economictimes.indiatimes.com/magazines/panache/robots-help-children-with-autism-boost-their-social-skills/articleshow/82195081.cms?utm_source=contentofinterest&utm_medium=text&utm_campaign=cppst
5.   https://www.softbankrobotics.com/emea/en/nao
6.   https://www.wired.com/story/what-is-a-robot/
7.   https://syntouchinc.com
8.   https://www.mckinsey.com/business-functions/operations/our-insights/automation-robotics-and-the-factory-of-the-future
9.   https://news.umich.edu/package-delivery-robots-environmental-impacts-automation-matters-less-than-vehicle-type/
10. https://www.transparencymarketresearch.com/robotics-software-platforms-market.html#:%7E:text=The%20robotics%20software%20platform%20market%20constitute%20established%20OEMs,for%20research%20and%20experiment%20on%20robots%20for%20simulation.
11. https://www.hansonrobotics.com/sophia/
12. https://cs.stanford.edu/people/eroberts/courses/soco/projects/1998-99/robotics/history.html
13. https://asimo.honda.com/
14. https://www.digitaltrends.com/cool-tech/top-10-robots-ever-built/
15. https://www.automate.org/a3-content/joseph-engelberger-unimate
16. https://newatlas.com/shakey-robot-sri-fiftieth-anniversary/37668/#:%7E:text=Shakey%20was%20described%20in%20Life%20magazine%20in%201970,tale%20about%20overestimating%20the%20state%20of%20the%20art.
17. https://www.nms.ac.uk/explore-our-collections/stories/science-and-technology/freddy-the-robot/
18. https://www.wired.com/story/wired-guide-to-robots/
19. https://robots.ieee.org/robots/genghis/
20. https://www.digitaltrends.com/cool-tech/turtle-mars-rover-kickstarter/
21. https://www.youtube.com/watch?v=PHWcBbf0Eng

22. https://www.digitaltrends.com/home/irobot-announces-new-roomba-and-smartphone-app/
23. https://www.digitaltrends.com/cool-tech/boston-dynamics-bigdog-can-now-hurl-cinderblocks/
24. https://www.bcg.com/publications/2021/how-intelligence-and-mobility-will-shape-the-future-of-the-robotics-industry#:%7E:text=Robotics%20is%20a%20crowded%20industry%20of%20more%20than,and%20small%20loads%20in%20logistics%20or%20assembly%20lines.
25. https://www.mckinsey.com/business-functions/operations/our-insights/automation-robotics-and-the-factory-of-the-future
26. https://www.forbes.com/sites/anniebrown/2021/07/04/ai-driven-robots-are-here-for-good/?sh=51c2aec94
27. https://www.thebusinessresearchcompany.com/press-release/top-robotics-market-2022
28. https://www.globenewswire.com/en/news-release/2022/05/25/2450099/0/en/The-Global-Industrial-Robotics-Market-size-was-valued-at-USD-32-32-billion-in-2021-and-is-predicted-to-reach-USD-88-55-billion-by-2030-with-a-CAGR-of-12-1-from-2022-2030.html
29. https://www.thebusinessresearchcompany.com/press-release/top-robotics-market-2022
30. https://www.idtechex.com/en/research-report/mobile-robots-autonomous-vehicles-and-drones-in-logistics-warehousing-and-delivery-2020-2040/706
31. https://www.idtechex.com/en/research-report/mobile-robots-autonomous-vehicles-and-drones-in-logistics-warehousing-and-delivery-2020-2040/706
32. https://www.forbes.com/sites/amyfeldman/2021/03/12/robotics-firms-garnered-63-billion-in-venture-funding-during-the-pandemic-year/?sh=33623ad93c1a
33. https://www.globenewswire.com/en/news-release/2022/05/25/2450099/0/en/The-Global-Industrial-Robotics-Market-size-was-valued-at-USD-32-32-billion-in-2021-and-is-predicted-to-reach-USD-88-55-billion-by-2030-with-a-CAGR-of-12-1-from-2022-2030.html
34. https://www.mordorintelligence.com/industry-reports/robotics-market
35. https://www.roboticstomorrow.com/article/2019/12/autonomous-mobile-robots-in-warehouses-idtechex-asks-what-justifies-the-recent-high-valuations/14611
36. https://www.roboticstomorrow.com/article/2019/12/autonomous-mobile-robots-in-warehouses-idtechex-asks-what-justifies-the-recent-high-valuations/14611
37. https://www.mordorintelligence.com/industry-reports/robotics-market
38. https://www.globenewswire.com/en/news-release/2022/05/03/2434212/28124/en/Global-Medical-Robotics-Market-Report-2022-Market-will-Reach-30-41-Billion-in-2027-from-US-9-69-Billion-in-2021.html
39. https://www.globenewswire.com/en/news-release/2022/05/03/2434212/28124/en/Global-Medical-Robotics-Market-Report-2022-Market-will-Reach-30-41-Billion-in-2027-from-US-9-69-Billion-in-2021.html
40. https://www.forbes.com/sites/amyfeldman/2021/03/12/robotics-firms-garnered-63-billion-in-venture-funding-during-the-pandemic-year/?sh=3c1420133c1a
41. https://www.forbes.com/sites/amyfeldman/2021/03/12/robotics-firms-garnered-63-billion-in-venture-funding-during-the-pandemic-year/?sh=55ef3f453c1a
42. https://www.idtechex.com/en/research-report/mobile-robots-autonomous-vehicles-and-drones-in-logistics-warehousing-and-delivery-2020-2040/706
43. https://www.businesswire.com/news/home/20210408005466/en/Global-Agricultural-Robots-Market-2021-to-2026---Industry-Trends-Share-Size-Growth-Opportunity-and-Forecasts---ResearchAndMarkets.com
44. https://www.idtechex.com/en/research-report/mobile-robots-autonomous-vehicles-and-drones-in-logistics-warehousing-and-delivery-2020-2040/706
45. https://www.globenewswire.com/en/news-release/2021/08/18/2282768/0/en/Global-Robotics-Market-Growth-Trends-COVID-19-Impact-and-Forecasts-2021-2026.html
46. https://www.reportlinker.com/p06129730/Global-Robotics-Market-Growth-Trends-COVID-19-Impact-and-Forecasts.html
47. https://markets.businessinsider.com/news/stocks/be-intelligent-about-automation-register-for-blue-prism-world-1030308292#:%7E:text=Automation%20has%20only%20just%20begun%20to%20show%20its,to%20be%20inspired%20to%20achieve%20true%20digital%20transformation.
48. https://www.businesswire.com/news/home/20210419005583/en/Global-Robotics-Market-2020-to-2026---by-Component-Type-End-user-and-Region---ResearchAndMarkets.com
49. https://www.forbes.com/sites/amyfeldman/2021/03/12/robotics-firms-garnered-63-billion-in-venture-funding-during-the-pandemic-year/?sh=33623ad93c1a
50. https://www.thebusinessresearchcompany.com/press-release/top-robotics-market-2022
51. https://www.globenewswire.com/en/news-release/2022/06/03/2455910/0/en/Global-Service-Robotics-Market-Size-Share-Industry-Trends-Analysis-Report-By-Application-By-Environment-By-Type-By-Component-By-Hardware-Type-By-Regional-Outlook-and-Forecast-2022-.html
52. https://greencleanguide.com/how-robotics-is-revolutionizing-sustainability/
53. https://www.skygrow.com.au/solution
54. https://www.urbanriv.org/in-the-news
55. https://www.evolving-science.com/intelligent-machines-robotics-automation-transportation/meet-ocean-one-humanoid-robot-exploring-our
56. https://www.bbntimes.com/technology/how-green-robots-are-helping-with-environmental-sustainability
57. https://www.fastcompany.com/3052893/this-swimming-robot-digests-pollution-and-turns-it-into-electricity
58. https://www.wastetodaymagazine.com/article/recycling-robots-ai-sorting/
59. https://www.wastetodaymagazine.com/article/recon-services-construction-demolition-recycling-operations/
60. https://www.quincycompressor.com/how-a-pneumatic-robot-arm-works/
61. https://www.cnet.com/tech/mobile/how-apples-daisy-iphone-recycling-robot-works/
62. https://www.amprobotics.com/our-purpose
63. https://flex.com/company/our-sustainability
64. https://greencleanguide.com/how-robotics-is-revolutionizing-sustainability/
65. https://www.drugwatch.com/davinci-surgery/
66. https://www.nextbigfuture.com/2018/05/suitx-lowers-cost-of-full-body-medical-mobility-exoskeleton-to-40000.html
67. https://www.mordorintelligence.com/industry-reports/robotics-market
68. https://digital-strategy.ec.europa.eu/en/news/danish-disinfection-robots-save-lives-fight-against-corona-virus
69. https://robotsforgood.yale.edu
70. https://www.rethinkrobotics.com
71. https://www.hahn.group/en/
72. https://www.rethinkrobotics.com/sawyer
73. https://www.cobotteam.com
74. https://www.researchgate.net/publication/314491851_One_hundred_years_of_clinical_laboratory_automation_1967-2067
75. https://www.researchgate.net/publication/319491544_Gerontechnology_Domotics_and_Robotics

76. https://www.asme.org/topics-resources/content/10-humanoid-robots-of-2020
77. https://www.lifescience-robotics.com
78. https://www.businesswire.com/news/home/20210712005530/en/Global-Educational-Robot-Market-2021-to-2026---Industry-Trends-Share-Size-Growth-Opportunity-and-Forecasts---ResearchAndMarkets.com
79. https://www.mhi.org/fundamentals/robots
80. https://www.therobotreport.com/robotics-iot-sustain-triple-bottom-line/
81. https://d6labs.com
82. https://www.weforum.org/agenda/2021/08/bees-hive-shelter-pollinators-insects-agriculture-tech
83. https://www.nature.com/articles/d41586-019-02007-7?proof=t+target=&error=cookies_not_supported&code=e2d5656b-8e92-441b-837a-bf9e0762545e
84. https://smprobotics.com/about_smp_robotics_company/
85. https://www.sciencedirect.com/science/article/pii/S0167865517301198
86. https://apera.io/p/robot-as-a-service-raas-business-models-in-the-mar
87. https://venturebeat.com/2019/06/30/the-rise-of-robots-as-a-service/
88. https://www.roboticsbusinessreview.com/manufacturing/designing-robots-service-model/
89. https://www.cnbc.com/2018/03/30/cobalt-raises-more-than-16-million-to-bring-security-robots-to-the-office.html
90. https://www.globenewswire.com/en/news-release/2022/03/14/2402758/0/en/At-16-5-CAGR-Global-Robot-as-a-Service-RaaS-Market-Size-Share-worth-USD-44-Billion-by-2028-Service-Robotics-Industry-Trends-Forecast-Report-by-Facts-Factors.html
91. https://www.forbes.com/sites/anniebrown/2021/07/04/ai-driven-robots-are-here-for-good/?sh=51c2aec94daf
92. https://www.mckinsey.com/about-us/new-at-mckinsey-blog/a-peek-into-the-future-of-surgery
93. https://www.distalmotion.com/product/
94. https://health.economictimes.indiatimes.com/news/medical-devices/google-teams-with-johnson-johnson-on-robotic-surgery/46722224
95. https://trends.medicalexpo.com/project-431373.html
96. https://aethon.com/mobile-robots-for-healthcare/
97. https://trends.medicalexpo.com/project-431373.html
98. https://www.mdpi.com/2218-6581/10/1/47/htm
99. https://www.blue-ocean-robotics.com
100. https://uvd.blue-ocean-robotics.com
101. https://spectrum.ieee.org/autonomous-robots-are-helping-kill-coronavirus-in-hospitals
102. https://www.intelligentliving.co/smart-field-hospital-robots-china/
103. https://www.intelligentliving.co/virus-killing-uvd-robots/
104. https://jmvh.org/article/glimpses-of-future-battlefield-medicine-the-proliferation-of-robotic-surgeons-and-unmanned-vehicles-and-technologies/
105. https://jmvh.org/article/glimpses-of-future-battlefield-medicine-the-proliferation-of-robotic-surgeons-and-unmanned-vehicles-and-technologies/
106. https://jmvh.org/article/glimpses-of-future-battlefield-medicine-the-proliferation-of-robotic-surgeons-and-unmanned-vehicles-and-technologies/
107. https://www.medstarfranklinsquare.org/our-services/surgical-services/treatments/robotic-surgery/benefits-of-robotic-surgery/
108. https://us.aibo.com/feature/ai.html
109. https://www.mordorintelligence.com/industry-reports/robotics-market
110. http://www.bocco.me/bocco-emo/#about
111. https://furhatrobotics.com
112. https://www2.deloitte.com/nl/nl/pages/over-deloitte/articles/alice.html
113. https://vu.nl/en/research/a-good-conversation-with-alice-the-robot
114. https://www.alicecares.nl/about-alice
115. https://www.holoniq.com/notes/2019-robotics-report/
116. https://sphero.com/blogs/news/sphero-littlebits-join-forces
117. https://marketbrief.edweek.org/marketplace-k-12/report-predicts-growing-demand-educational-robotics-worldwide/#:%7E:text=Robotics%20used%20in%20education%20will%20continue%20to%20be,according%20to%20findings%20by%20market%20research%20firm%20HolonIQ.
118. https://www.holoniq.com/notes/2019-robotics-report/
119. https://www.vexrobotics.com/competition?___store=vexroboticseu&___from_store=vexrobotics
120. https://thebrainary.com/fable/
121. https://shop.miko3.ai/blogs/news/the-first-miko-family-huddle-in-brief
122. https://owllabs.com/industry/healthcare
123. https://www.wiglbot.com
124. https://edition.cnn.com/2020/09/02/investing/lego-sales-pandemic-trnd/index.html
125. https://www.lego.com/en-us
126. https://education.lego.com/en-us/products/lego-education-spike-prime-set/45678#lego-learning-system
127. https://www.forbes.com/sites/dereknewton/2020/02/08/lego-is-probably-the-biggest-education-company-on-earth/?sh=7a3429fe478c#:~:text=The%20company's%20annual%20revenues%20surpass%20%245%20billion%20and,probably%20the%20biggest%20education%20company%20in%20the%20world.
128. https://www.idtech.com/blog/best-coding-toys-for-kids
129. https://www.forbes.com/sites/kathryndill/2015/02/19/lego-tops-global-ranking-of-the-most-powerful-brands-in-2015/?sh=4a75a08626f0
130. https://www.dobot.cc/customer-story/dobot-robot-kits-incorporated-at-mechatronics-engineering-lab-rajamangala-university-of-technology-lanna.html
131. https://www.mistyrobotics.com/use-cases/misty-ii-your-partner-in-university-education-and-research/
132. https://www.sdu.dk/en/forskning/sdurobotics/sdg
133. https://www.greengrowthknowledge.org/research/value-land-quick-guide-report
134. https://www.greengrowthknowledge.org/research/value-land-quick-guide-report
135. https://wyss.harvard.edu/news/laying-the-ground-for-robotic-strategies-in-environmental-protection/
136. https://wyss.harvard.edu/news/saving-the-planet-with-robots-microbes-and-nanotechnology/
137. https://www.fastcompany.com/3052893/this-swimming-robot-digests-pollution-and-turns-it-into-electricity
138. https://americansforbgu.org/lizard-inspired-robot/#
139. https://www.syfy.com/syfy-wire/amphibious-robot-patterned-after-lizards-and-roaches
140. https://www.epfl.ch/labs/biorob/research/amphibious/amphibot/
141. https://www.epfl.ch/en/
142. https://ideas.ted.com/this-amazing-robot-swims-like-an-eel-and-detects-pollution/
143. https://ec.europa.eu/research-and-innovation/en/horizon-magazine/robot-bees-open-lid-hive-behaviour
144. https://www.weforum.org/agenda/2018/03/autonomous-robot-bees-are-being-patented-by-walmart
145. https://www.sciencedirect.com/science/article/pii/S1474667016334942
146. https://www.sciencedirect.com/science/article/pii/S1474667016334942

147. https://www.allerin.com/blog/how-green-robots-are-helping-with-environmental-sustainability
148. https://www.forbes.com/sites/robtoews/2021/06/20/these-are-the-startups-applying-ai-to-tackle-climate-change/?sh=56e-7a8937b26
149. https://www.naio-technologies.com/en/naio-technologies/
150. https://techxplore.com/news/2021-06-robot-farmerswith-responsible-developmentcould-jobs.html
151. https://sagarobotics.com
152. https://www.energid.com/industries/agricultural-robotics
153. https://interestingengineering.com/9-robots-that-are-invading-the-agriculture-industry
154. https://research.reading.ac.uk/research-blog/robot-farmers-could-improve-jobs-and-help-fight-climate-change-if-theyre-developed-responsibly/
155. https://www.weforum.org/agenda/2020/08/here-s-how-robots-can-help-us-confront-covid/
156. https://www.industrialtechnology.co.uk/news/products
157. https://linkinghub.elsevier.com/retrieve/pii/S2351978917300628
158. https://www.weforum.org/agenda/2020/08/here-s-how-robots-can-help-us-confront-covid/
159. https://www.ge.com/research/technology-domains/robotics-autonomous-systems
160. https://blog.robotiq.com/the-10-sustainability-benefits-to-choosing-robot-finishing
161. https://techcrunch.com/2021/09/14/locus-robotics-just-raised-another-50m/
162. https://www.forbes.com/sites/amyfeldman/2021/02/17/meet-the-newest-robotics-unicorn-locus-robotics-raises-150-million-at-1-billion-valuation-on-surging-ecommerce-sales/?sh=241c0b0b1035
163. https://locusrobotics.com
164. https://aimagazine.com/ai-applications/ensuring-safety-in-warehouses-with-locus-robotics
165. https://www.forbes.com/sites/amyfeldman/2021/02/17/meet-the-newest-robotics-unicorn-locus-robotics-raises-150-million-at-1-billion-valuation-on-surging-ecommerce-sales/
166. https://ai-techpark.com/svt-robotics-and-locus-robotics-to-accelerate-amr-integration/
167. https://ifr.org
168. https://fanuc.co.jp/eindex.html
169. https://fanuc.co.jp/en/sustainability/sdgs/robotbusiness.html
170. https://techxplore.com/news/2021-06-robot-farmerswith-responsible-developmentcould-jobs.html
171. https://roboticsshop.net/advantages-and-disadvantages-of-robots-in-the-workplace/

Chapter 5: Advanced Materials

1. https://www.smithsonianmag.com/innovation/smog-eating-buildings-battle-air-pollution-1
2. http://www.prosolve370e.com/
3. https://www.nature.com/subjects/materials-science
4. https://www.icl-group.com/blog/what-are-advanced-materials-industrial-applications/
5. https://www.nytimes.com/2021/04/27/science/metamaterials-technology.html
6. https://spectrum.ieee.org/video/semiconductors/materials/looking-ahead-4-tomorrows-materials#:~:text=The+most+promising+jewel+in+this+arena+is,conductivity.+It's+the+stuff+legends+are+made+of.
7. https://spectrum.ieee.org/video/semiconductors/materials/looking-ahead-4-tomorrows-materials#:~:text=The+most+promising+jewel+in+this+arena+is,conductivity.+It's+the+stuff+legends+are+made+of.
8. https://www.sciencedirect.com/topics/biochemistry-genetics-and-molecular-biology/combinatorial-chemistry
9. https://www.theregister.com/2019/07/16/aerogel_mars_shelters/
10. https://www.youtube.com/watch?v=SkM_1Pdj8xM
11. https://beckman.illinois.edu
12. https://www.nature.com/articles/s41586-019-1074-x
13. https://www.thomasnet.com/insights/these-5-innovative-materials-are-changing-the-world/#:~:text=Their%20corrugated%20structure%20means%20the%20charged%20ions%20in,from%20hard-to-source%20lithium%20ions%20to%20abundant%20sodium%20ions.
14. https://www.thomasnet.com/insights/tesla-warns-of-lithium-ion-battery-mineral-shortage/
15. https://phys.org/news/2019-04-accidentally-material-revolutionise-batteries-electronics.html
16. https://spectrum.ieee.org/video/semiconductors/materials/looking-ahead-4-tomorrows-materials#:~:text=The+most+promising+jewel+in+this+arena+is,conductivity.+It's+the+stuff+legends+are+made+of.
17. https://dozr.com/blog/bessemer-process
18. https://archetype.co.uk/our-titles/east-asian-lacquer/?id=4
19. https://www.tec-science.com/material-science/structure-of-metals/crystallographic-defects/
20. https://www.goldsteinresearch.com/report/global-advanced-materials-market
21. https://www.goldsteinresearch.com/report/global-advanced-materials-market
22. https://www.industryarc.com/Report/15380/advanced-materials-market.html
23. https://www.industryarc.com/Report/15380/advanced-materials-market.html
24. https://www.marketwatch.com/press-release/global-advanced-materials-market-size-share-and-growth-to-bolster-at-10-cagr-through-2025-2021-05-31
25. https://www.researchnester.com/reports/advanced-materials-market/448
26. https://www.researchandmarkets.com/reports/4594086/global-advanced-materials-market-outlook-2024
27. https://www.researchandmarkets.com/reports/4594086/global-advanced-materials-market-outlook-2024
28. https://www.researchnester.com/reports/advanced-materials-market/448
29. https://www.researchandmarkets.com/reports/4594086/global-advanced-materials-market-outlook-2024
30. https://www.industryarc.com/Report/15380/advanced-materials-market.html
31. https://www.marketwatch.com/press-release/global-advanced-materials-market-size-share-and-growth-to-bolster-at-10-cagr-through-2025-2021-05-31
32. https://www.verifiedmarketresearch.com/product/algae-market/
33. https://www.researchandmarkets.com/reports/4594086/global-advanced-materials-market-outlook-2024
34. www.alliedmarketresearch.com/advanced-building-materials-market-A16498
35. https://www.globaldata.com/store/report/advanced-materials-theme-analysis/
36. https://www.industryarc.com/Report/15380/advanced-materials-market.html
37. https://www.industryarc.com/Report/15380/advanced-materials-market.html
38. https://www.industryarc.com/Report/15380/advanced-materials-market.html
39. https://www.marketwatch.com/press-release/global-advanced-materials-market-size-share-and-growth-to-bolster-at-10-cagr-through-2025-2021-05-31

40. https://www.researchandmarkets.com/reports/4594086/global-advanced-materials-market-outlook-2024
41. https://www.earlycharm.com
42. https://www.earlycharm.com
43. https://matericgroup.com/nanodirect-joins-set-of-advanced-materials-companies-to-launch-materic-llc/
44. https://matericgroup.com
45. https://www.bcs.org/content-hub/10-disruptive-technologies-and-how-they-ll-change-your-life/
46. https://doi.org/10.1002/btpr.3179
47. https://www.newscientist.com/article/dn13420-floppy-when-wet-sea-cucumber-inspires-new-plastic/
48. https://static1.squarespace.com/static/5b9362d89d5abb8c51d-474f8/t/5d9fbb05347a600a899c63e7/1570749191805/Carbon-tech+Fact+Sheet+2019+Final+%28Print%29.pdf
49. https://www.carbfix.com
50. https://www.bloomberg.com/news/articles/2021-03-05/bill-gates-investment-in-carbon-removal-tech
51. https://www.carbfix.com/how-it-works
52. https://www.carbfix.com/carbfix-atlas-old
53. https://fortune.com/2021/03/06/carbon-capture-storage-rocks-net-zero-carbfix-startup-iceland/
54. https://www.crunchbase.com/organization/carbfix/company_overview/overview_timeline
55. https://www.azonano.com/article.aspx?ArticleID=5597
56. http://strigiformes.pl/produkt/bio-agrovita-plus/
57. https://www.solvay.com/en/press-release/solvay-partners-mitsubishi-chemical-advanced-materials-recycle-end-life-medical
58. https://www.solvay.com/en/sustainability
59. https://www.arkema.com/global/en/?_ga=-GA1.1.1549414966.1658251936
60. https://www.researchgate.net/publication/313236664_Smart_Materials_for_Smart_Cities_and_Sustainable_Environment
61. https://dexmat.com
62. https://www.houston.org/news/major-local-academic-institutions-companies-growing-houstons-advanced-materials-sector
63. https://a2oadvancedmaterials.com
64. https://oceanstartupproject.ca/a2o/
65. https://www.mdpi.com/1422-0067/23/14/7980/htm
66. https://www.nanowerk.com/what_are_quantum_dots.php
67. https://www.youtube.com/watch?v=JeaocXPmYtQ
68. https://www.globaldata.com/store/report/advanced-materials-theme-analysis/
69. https://www.sciencedirect.com/science/article/pii/S0360319919304057
70. https://www.energy.gov/eere/vehicles/lightweight-materials-cars-and-trucks
71. https://nanolumi.com
72. https://nanolumi.com/technology/
73. https://nanolumi.com/product/
74. https://www.elsevier.com/__data/assets/pdf_file/0018/120942/R_D-Solutions_CHEM_Ebook_Advanced-Materials_DIGITAL.pdf
75. https://doi.org/10.1007/s42452-018-0054-3
76. https://intelligence.weforum.org/topics/a1Gb0000001j9vgE-AA?tab=publications
77. https://www.opusmaterialstechnologies.com
78. https://www.grandviewresearch.com/industry-analysis/battery-market
79. https://www.nature.com/articles/s41467-020-19850-2
80. https://news.mit.edu/2020/cool-advance-thermoelectric-conversion-1211
81. https://www.polarismarketresearch.com/industry-analysis/carbon-capture-and-storage-market
82. https://solcold.co
83. https://www.exitvalley.com/Projects/solcold/?WebLang=EN
84. https://www.exitvalley.com/Projects/solcold/?WebLang=EN
85. https://www.nature.com/articles/s41586-020-2495-2.epdf?sharing_token=MLgynzEFNTjMq-xaHYWbstRgN0jAjWel9jnR-3ZoTv0PR9RVMKXRwBK8FcQPIUiO95IHiJsS1-KY2zV1GbO-39YuX6_Ir8IingnYP21n9L1fv9xgPq2KCZZoh_IQuoIESoJP9o-vf13uYEjywytv9Q9CPgpt6bmvE2qXJfCYKdLVNQ%3D
86. https://researchreportsworld.com/2021-2027-global-and-regional-recyclable-thermosets-industry-status-and-prospects-professional-market-18109798
87. https://ionicindustries.com.au/
88. https://www.techconnectworld.com/World2016/show-case/?action=viewmaturity&maturity=Commercial%20Product
89. https://climate.mit.edu/posts/chemists-make-tough-plastics-recyclable
90. https://www.industryprotomold.com/dcpd-process-intruduction/
91. https://ionicindustries.com.au/wp-content/uploads/2020/11/2011-AGM-Presentation.pdf
92. https://www.mckinsey.com/industries/life-sciences/our-insights/rethinking-manufacturing-and-distribution-networks-in-medtech
93. https://www.mynusco.com
94. https://mynusco.com/mynusco-indian-start-up-pioneers-bio-material-platform-to-fight-climate-change-ibc-world-news/
95. https://www.spectalite.com/
96. https://mynusco.com/biodur-biocomposites/
97. https://mynusco.com/biopur-biocomposites/
98. https://intelligence.weforum.org/topics/a1Gb0000001j9vgE-AA?tab=publications
99. https://www.ncbi.nlm.nih.gov/pmc/articles/PMC8781893/
100. https://nobel-project.eu/technologies-in-medtech/nanotechnologies-for-healthcare/
101. https://nobel-project.eu/technologies-in-medtech/nanotechnologies-for-healthcare/
102. https://www.mayo.edu/research/centers-programs/center-regenerative-medicine/about/about-regenerative-medicine https://faculty.ksu.edu.sa/en/aalshamsan/page/78037
103. https://faculty.ksu.edu.sa/en/aalshamsan/page/78037
104. https://nobel-project.eu/technologies-in-medtech/nanotechnologies-for-healthcare/
105. https://www.researchgate.net/publication/256443316_A_review_of_nanotechnology_development_in_the_Arab_World
106. https://www.lexology.com/library/detail.aspx?g=46301531-6586-4ad6-965d-8a5b811c3e46
107. https://industrial.honeywell.com/us/en/applications/cut-resistant-fibers-and-materials/rope/spectra-fiber
108. https://www.mpo-mag.com/contents/view_online-exclusives/2020-06-02/new-materials-impact-the-medical-technology-outsourcing-market/
109. https://www.wfp.org/stories/5-facts-about-food-waste-and-hunger
110. https://www.who.int/news/item/06-07-2022-un-report--global-hunger-numbers-rose-to-as-many-as-828-million-in-2021
111. https://www.rubicon.com/blog/food-waste-facts/
112. https://www.aamc.org/news-insights/54-million-people-america-face-food-insecurity-during-pandemic-it-could-have-dire-consequences-their
113. https://pangaeaventures.com/portfolio
114. https://pangaeaventures.com/_documents/Pangaea%20Ventures%202020%20Impact%20Report.pdf add endnote
115. http://www.stixfreshindia.com
116. https://www.ryplabs.com/stixfresh
117. https://www.wfp.org/stories/5-facts-about-food-waste-and-hunger
118. https://www2.deloitte.com/content/dam/Deloitte/de/Documents/consumer-industrial-products/Deloitte-Transformation-from-Agriculture-to-AgTech-2016.pdf

119. https://www.croplife.com/management/agtech-venture-capital-roundup-an-overview-of-startup-funding-in-2020-and-what-to-expect-in-2021/
120. https://www.waste360.com/food-waste/oprah-winfrey-and-katy-perry-invest-food-waste-solutions-apeel-science
121. https://www.waste360.com/food-waste/oprah-winfrey-and-katy-perry-invest-food-waste-solutions-apeel-science
122. https://www.croplife.com/management/agtech-venture-capital-roundup-an-overview-of-startup-funding-in-2020-and-what-to-expect-in-2021/
123. https://www.croplife.com/management/agtech-venture-capital-roundup-an-overview-of-startup-funding-in-2020-and-what-to-expect-in-2021/
124. https://www.mosaicco.com/Sustainability-Reporting
125. https://s1.q4cdn.com/823038994/files/doc_financials/2021/q1/1Q21-News-Release-FINAL.pdf
126. https://www.hazeltechnologies.com
127. https://www.forbes.com/sites/robindschatz/2021/04/13/hazel-technologies-food-waste-solutions-get-70-million-boost/?sh=313ed6db15ae
128. https://thespoon.tech/hazel-technologies-raises-70m-in-series-c-funding-to-fight-food-waste/
129. https://www.cleantech.com/recent-deals-27-april/
130. https://www.advancedmaterialsworld.com/articles/22726/webinar-smart-cities-the-400bn-opportunity-for-advanced-materials
131. https://www.idtechex.com/en/research-report/smart-cities-emerging-materials-markets-2021-2041/792
132. https://www.idtechex.com/en/research-article/smart-city-materials-400-billion-market/22586
133. https://www.advancedmaterialsworld.com/articles/22726/webinar-smart-cities-the-400bn-opportunity-for-advanced-materials
134. http://concretehelper.com/concrete-facts/
135. https://www.specifyconcrete.org/blog/eco-friendly-alternatives-to-traditional-concrete
136. https://cfotech.co.nz/story/advanced-materials-for-smart-cities-valued-as-400bn-market
137. https://www.agc-multimaterial.com/company/
138. https://www.who.int/airpollution/data/cities-2016/en/
139. https://theconstructor.org/concrete/smog-eating-concrete-buildings-pollution/57052/
140. https://architizer.com/blog/inspiration/industry/smog-eating-facades-and-the-future-of-our-air-quality/
141. https://www.grandviewresearch.com/industry-analysis/textile-market
142. https://www.textileworld.com/textile-world/features/2020/05/new-developments-in-fibers-yarns-fabrics/
143. https://goodfair.com/blogs/nonewthings/did-you-know-that-one-t-shirt-guzzles-over-700-gallons-of-water#:~:text=To%20make%20one%20cotton%20T,30%20miles%20in%20the%20U.S.
144. https://solve.mit.edu/articles/how-this-brilliant-entrepreneur-is-turning-textile-waste-into-business-profit
145. https://www.solvay.com/en/
146. https://www.solvay.com/sites/g/files/srpend221/files/2022-06/Solvay%20Today%202022%20-%20EN.pdf
147. https://www.solvay.com/en/solutions-market/agriculture-feed/crop-protection
148. https://www.solvay.com/en/solutions-market/agriculture-feed/crop-protection/biopesticides/products
149. https://cen.acs.org/business/finance/CENs-Global-Top-50-2022/100/i26
150. https://www.marketwatch.com/press-release/textile-enzymes-market-2021---market-share-top-manufacturers-globally-market-size-and-forecast-to-2027-with-top-growth-companies-2021-03-18
151. https://www.fastcompany.com/90395845/5-wild-organic-materials-that-could-transform-the-fashion-industry
152. https://www.marketwatch.com/press-release/textile-enzymes-market-2021---market-share-top-manufacturers-globally-market-size-and-forecast-to-2027-with-top-growth-companies-2021-03-18
153. https://news.climate.columbia.edu/2021/06/10/why-fashion-needs-to-be-more-sustainable/
154. https://news.climate.columbia.edu/2021/06/10/why-fashion-needs-to-be-more-sustainable/
155. https://www.textileworld.com/textile-world/features/2020/05/new-developments-in-fibers-yarns-fabrics/
156. https://www.bbcearth.com/news/six-fashion-materials-that-could-help-save-the-planet
157. https://www.lenzing.com/products/tenceltm
158. https://www.anthropocenemagazine.org/2021/05/algae-could-help-make-the-fashion-industry-green/
159. https://www.jhuapl.edu/Content/techdigest/pdf/V21-N04/21-04-Rooney.pdf
160. https://www.agc.com/en/
161. https://www.agc-multimaterial.com/company/
162. https://agc-activeglass.com/en/sunewat/
163. https://agc-activeglass.com/en/projects/hikari-building-lyon/
164. https://agc-activeglass.com/en/projects/hikari-building-lyon/
165. https://www.agc-glass.eu/en/news/blog-article/glass-creating-positive-energy-more-ways-one
166. https://sst.semiconductor-digest.com/2017/07/new-materials-new-challenges/
167. https://bohatala.com/advantages-and-disadvantages-of-graphene/
168. https://notesmatic.com/applications-advantages-and-disadvantages-of-nanotechnology/
169. https://www.ananas-anam.com
170. https://www.ananas-anam.com/worlds-first-vegan-hotel-suite-opens-at-the-hilton-bankside-london-featuring-pinatex-as-its-core-material/
171. https://www.thenationalnews.com/lifestyle/travel/inside-london-s-first-all-vegan-suite-at-the-hilton-london-bankside-hotel-1.839001
172. https://www.hilton.com/en/book/reservation/rates/
173. https://www.standard.co.uk/lifestyle/the-world-s-first-vegan-hotel-suite-has-come-to-london-a4045741.html
174. https://mcusercontent.com/03e5e1519304764711156f2f5/files/dc3e7091-8e16-c56a-44d0-e422d04af27a/Ananas_Anam_Impact_Report_2021.01.pdf
175. https://vegconomist.com/fashion-design-and-beauty/dole-sunshine-company-worlds-largest-producer-of-fruit-veg-partners-with-ananas-anam-to-upcycle-pineapple-waste/

Chapter 6: Extended Realities

1. https://www.accenture.com/us-en/insights/technology/immersive-learning
2. https://maestrolearning.com/blogs/is-ar-vr-technology-a-better-way-to-learn-heres-the-latest-research/
3. https://childrenstreatmentcenter.com/autistic-children-virtual-reality-therapy/#:~:text=How%20Can%20VR%20Therapy%20Help%20Autistic%20Children%3F%20Among,with%20autism%20become%20more%20comfortable%20in%20social%20settings.
4. https://pediatrics.jmir.org/2019/2/e14429/
5. http://www.neurociencies.ub.edu/virtual-reality-to-help-solve-personal-problems/
6. https://techterms.com/definition/augmented_reality
7. https://techterms.com/definition/virtualreality
8. https://docs.microsoft.com/en-us/windows/mixed-reality/discover/mixed-reality#the-mixed-reality-spectrum

9. https://www.microsoft.com/en-us/hololens
10. https://www.researchgate.net/publication/231514051_A_Taxonomy_of_Mixed_Reality_Visual_Displays
11. https://www.cmswire.com/digital-workplace/why-facebooks-metaverse-is-still-only-a-pipedream/
12. https://bernardmarr.com/what-is-the-metaverse-an-easy-explanation-for-anyone/
13. https://www.unicef.org/innovation/XR
14. https://breakthrough.unglobalcompact.org/site/assets/files/1520/hhw-16-0026-d_b3_new_realities.pdf
15. https://www.weforum.org/agenda/2021/02/virtual-reality-augmented-reality-sustainable-development/
16. https://www.qualcomm.com/5g
17. https://www.qualcomm.com/snapdragon
18. https://www.qualcomm.com/products/snapdragon-xr2-5g-platform
19. https://www.mordorintelligence.com/industry-reports/extended-reality-xr-market
20. https://www.techadvisor.com/article/743826/oculus-quest-2-pro-all-you-need-to-know-about-project-cambria.html
21. https://vrscout.com/news/report-apple-mixed-reality-launching-2022/
22. https://www.brainbridge.be/news/get-ready-for-apples-new-8k-vrar-headset-in-2020
23. https://www.metavision.com
24. https://www.toptal.com/designers/product-design/vr-ar-mr-the-future-of-design
25. https://www.badvr.com
26. https://badvr.com/product/seesignal.html
27. https://techstartups.com/2019/07/11/los-angeles-startup-badvr-receives-grant-national-science-foundation-address-challenges-visualizing-analyzing-large-geospatial-data/
28. https://www.crunchbase.com/organization/badvr/company_financials
29. https://www.viavisolutions.com/es-es/literature/state-5g-deployments-2021-posters-en.pdf
30. https://my.ccsinsight.com/reportaction/D21748/Toc
31. https://www.globenewswire.com/news-release/2021/01/26/2154346/0/en/Worldwide-Extended-Reality-Industry-to-2025-COVID-19-May-Act-as-an-Opportunity-to-the-Industry.html
32. https://azure.microsoft.com/en-us/blog/hololens-2-expands-markets-azure-mixed-reality-services-now-broadly-available/
33. https://www.accenture.com/_acnmedia/accenture/redesign-assets/dotcom/documents/global/1/accenture-g20-yea-report.pdf
34. https://www.plm.automation.siemens.com/global/en/industries/automotive-transportation/automotive-oems/digital-mockup-virtual-augmented-reality.html
35. https://www.accenture.com/us-en/insights/technology/technology-trends-2021
36. https://azure.microsoft.com/en-us/overview/what-is-cloud-computing/#uses
37. https://azure.microsoft.com/en-us/overview/what-is-azure/?OCID=AID2200277_SEM_d3a481b6543a1d714bbee08d2dcf658f:G:s&ef_id=d3a481b6543a1d714bbee08d2dcf658f:G:s&msclkid=d3a481b6543a1d714bbee08d2dcf658f
38. https://azure.microsoft.com/en-us/overview/trusted-cloud/
39. https://mediartinnovation.com/2014/06/03/morton-heilig-sensorama-1957/
40. http://worrydream.com/refs/Sutherland%20-%20The%20Ultimate%20Display.pdf
41. https://www.dsource.in/course/virtual-reality-introduction/evolution-vr/sword-damocles-head-mounted-display
42. https://www.forbes.com/sites/bernardmarr/2021/05/17/the-fascinating-history-and-evolution-of-extended-reality-xr--covering-ar-vr-and-mr/?sh=33c336024bfd
43. https://www.imarcgroup.com/extended-reality-market
44. https://www.techrepublic.com/article/virtual-reality-a-cheat-sheet-for-business-pros/
45. https://www.marketsandmarkets.com/Market-Reports/augmented-reality-virtual-reality-market-1185.html
46. https://reports.valuates.com/market-reports/QYRE-Auto-7H1936/global-mixed-reality/#:~:text=MIXED%20REALITY%20MARKET%20STATISTICS%20The%20global%20Mixed%20Reality,real%20and%20virtual%20world%20object%20in%20real%20time.
47. https://www.mordorintelligence.com/industry-reports/extended-reality-xr-market
48. https://www.capgemini.com/wp-content/uploads/2018/09/AR-VR-in-Operations1.pdf
49. https://www.businesswire.com/news/home/20191217005455/en/Global-10.82-Billion-Healthcare-Augmented-Reality-Virtual
50. https://www.globenewswire.com/news-release/2020/12/29/2151082/0/en/The-extended-reality-market-is-projected-to-grow-from-42-55-billion-in-2020-to-333-16-billion-by-2025-at-a-CAGR-of-50-9-from-2020-to-2025.html
51. https://tesseract.in
52. https://developer.tesseract.in/#
53. https://www.siemens.com/global/en.html
54. https://www.vrdirect.com/blog/vr-for-training-hr/how-siemens-raises-employees-awareness-with-interactive-ehs-training/
55. https://jiotesseract.medium.com/6-5-billion-mixed-reality-industry-boom-in-india-by-2022-82900f4e65ed
56. https://www.transparencymarketresearch.com/extended-reality-xr-market.html
57. https://www.businesswire.com/news/home/20191217005455/en/Global-10.82-Billion-Healthcare-Augmented-Reality-Virtual
58. https://www.fortunebusinessinsights.com/industry-reports/virtual-reality-market-101378
59. https://ieeexplore.ieee.org/document/8699256
60. https://www.benjamindada.com/5g-deployment-in-nigeria/
61. https://atap.google.com/soli/
62. https://ict.usc.edu/prototypes/pts/
63. https://www.packagingdigest.com/smart-packaging/why-sustainably-minded-brands-use-augmented-reality
64. https://www.unicef.org/innovation/XR
65. https://www.pwc.com/gx/en/about/stories-from-across-the-world/visualising-solutions-for-the-un-sustainable-development-goals.html
66. https://www.climatecolab.org/contests/2017/shifting-attitudes-and-behavior/c/proposal/1334188
67. https://www.accuvein.com/
68. https://www.stgeorges.nhs.uk/newsitem/vr-headsets-relaxing-patients-during-surgery-at-st-georges/
69. https://www.weforum.org/agenda/2021/02/virtual-reality-augmented-reality-sustainable-development/
70. https://www.itu.int/en/ITU-D/Initiatives/GIGA/Pages/default.aspx
71. https://www.mondly.com/business
72. https://genderedinnovations.stanford.edu/case-studies/extendedVR.html#tabs-2
73. https://www.rem5vr.com
74. https://www.startribune.com/st-louis-park-virtual-reality-lab-aims-to-use-the-technology-for-more-than-just-entertainment/568441272/
75. https://www.weforum.org/agenda/2019/10/myanmar-gender-violence
76. https://www.maketecheasier.com/lenovo-introduces-smart-glasses-work-at-home-market/
77. https://www.lenovo.com/us/en/thinkrealitya3/
78. https://www.weforum.org/agenda/2021/02/virtual-reality-augmented-reality-sustainable-development/
79. https://www.qualcomm.com/research/extended-reality

80. https://www.qualcomm.com/research
81. https://www.authenticallyus.com
82. https://theprint.in/science/how-augmented-reality-can-help-create-sustainable-environment-friendly-smart-cities/349845/
83. https://www.nrf.gov.sg/programmes/virtual-singapore
84. https://www.govtech.com/smart-cities/digital-twin-technology-can-make-smart-cities-even-smarter.html
85. https://www.emergenresearch.com/blog/top-9-globally-leading-companies-in-the-extended-reality-market
86. https://breakthrough.unglobalcompact.org/site/assets/files/1520/hhw-16-0026-d_b3_new_realities.pdf
87. https://www.accenture.com/us-en/insights/technology/immersive-reality
88. https://www.forbes.com/sites/forbescommunicationscouncil/2018/04/17/augmented-reality-for-good/#363d7447ad1b
89. https://www.sytner.co.uk/audi/news/audi-vr-experience/
90. https://www.vuzix.com/solutions/warehouse
91. https://www.spheregen.com/extendedreality/
92. https://www.accenture.com/us-en/insights/technology/scaling-enterprise-digital-transformation
93. https://xra.org/wp-content/uploads/2021/02/XRA_Slicks_Healthcare_V2.pdf
94. https://www.spheregen.com/education/
95. https://rocketreach.co/spheregen-profile_b5ce5537f42e0977
96. https://www.ajog.org/action/consumeSharedSessionAction?J-SESSIONID=aaaVoqQus-vdg5UO45utx&MAID=Cy7yT9CK-jh%2B2z44O9bqqnw%3D%3D&SERVER=WZ6myaEXBLFK-jn1do9Q5dA%3D%3D&ORIGIN=190148371&RD=RD&rtc=0
97. https://www.forbes.com/sites/solrogers/2020/03/09/virtual-reality-for-good-use-cases-from-educating-on-racial-bias-to-pain-relief-during-childbirth/#64aebc9463f5
98. https://xra.org/wp-content/uploads/2021/02/XRA_Slicks_Healthcare_V2.pdf
99. http://www.aisolve.com/aisolves-chla-vr-pilot-simulation-expands-to-11-new-locations/
100. https://www.usa.philips.com/healthcare/resources/landing/azurion?npagination=1
101. https://www.accuvein.com/news/vein-visualization-emerges-as-premier-augmented-reality-application/
102. https://www.stgeorges.nhs.uk/newsitem/vr-headsets-relaxing-patients-during-surgery-at-st-georges/
103. https://www.stgeorges.nhs.uk/newsitem/vr-headsets-relaxing-patients-during-surgery-at-st-georges/
104. https://www.medivis.com
105. https://www.microsoft.com/en-us/hololens
106. https://techcrunch.com/2019/02/13/medivis-has-launched-its-augmented-reality-platform-for-surgical-planning/
107. https://www.medivis.com/surgicalar
108. https://www.microsoft.com/en-us/hololens/industry-healthcare
109. https://www.youtube.com/watch?v=1Ypovgka-9Q
110. https://teachers.tech/experiential-learning-augmented-reality-apps/
111. https://www.youtube.com/watch?v=1Ypovgka-9Q
112. https://arpost.co/2018/12/13/history-lovers-can-travel-to-ancient-rome-in-a-large-scale-virtual-reality-experience/
113. https://www.nasa.gov/stem-ed-resources/free-virtual-reality-program-nasa-sls-vr-experience.html
114. https://shipinsight.com/articles/mans-new-app-brings-ar-to-training
115. https://assets.new.siemens.com/siemens/assets/api/uuid:ca39bfe8-74e5-40d8-a18f-af93369c3ee9/comos-lifecycle-en.pdf#page=10
116. https://new.siemens.com/in/en/products/automation/industry-software/plant-engineering-software-comos/virtual-reality-training.html
117. https://theprint.in/science/how-augmented-reality-can-help-create-sustainable-environment-friendly-smart-cities/349845/
118. https://www.ijitee.org/wp-content/uploads/papers/v8i9S2/I10080789S219.pdf
119. https://www.media.mit.edu/articles/ar-is-transforming-tech-what-can-it-do-for-cities/
120. https://bernardmarr.com/10-best-examples-of-vr-and-ar-in-education/
121. https://www.amd.com/en
122. https://www.amd.com/en/corporate-responsibility/technology-classroom
123. https://www.amd.com/system/files/documents/vr-in-the-classroom-case-study.pdf
124. https://ir.amd.com/news-events/press-releases/detail/1044/amd-reports-fourth-quarter-and-full-year-2021-financial
125. https://transmira.com
126. https://www.mannpublications.com/mannreport/2021/04/08/transmira-kognition-team-to-develop-intelligent-architecture-smart-city-solutions/
127. https://www.mannpublications.com/mannreport/2021/04/08/transmira-kognition-team-to-develop-intelligent-architecture-smart-city-solutions/
128. https://thinkmobiles.com/blog/augmented-reality-retail/
129. https://www.magicleap.com/en-us
130. https://developer.apple.com/videos/play/wwdc2017/602/
131. https://www.reuters.com/article/us-tech-imagine-snapchat-idUSKBN14E06X
132. https://www.oculus.com
133. https://www.augment.com
134. https://vividworks.com
135. https://sayduck.com
136. https://financesonline.com/augmented-reality-trends/
137. https://www.projectarcher.com
138. https://thinkmobiles.com/blog/augmented-reality-retail/
139. https://www.oculus.com/vr-for-good/stories/mine-rescue-teams-discover-a-new-tool-for-training/
140. https://www.theguardian.com/travel/2021/jan/12/10-best-virtual-travel-experiences-2021-film-festivals-street-tours-wine-tasting
141. https://www.oculus.com/quest-2/
142. https://maryrose.org/panorama
143. https://projectdastaan.org
144. https://www.youtube.com/watch?v=-uqwpQLSkHY
145. https://projectdastaan.org
146. https://projectdastaan.org/about/
147. https://cancer.news/2020-02-05-why-5g-is-a-threat-to-overall-health.html
148. https://www.sciencedirect.com/science/article/abs/pii/S037842742030028X?via%3Dihub
149. https://sloanreview.mit.edu/article/preparing-for-the-risky-world-of-extended-reality/
150. https://www.accenture.com/_acnmedia/accenture/redesign-assets/dotcom/documents/global/1/accenture-g20-yea-report.pdf
151. https://www.science.org/lookup/doi/10.1126/science.aaw4399

Chapter 7: Autonomous Vehicles and Drones

1. https://mashable.com/article/drones-social-good-humanitarian-aid
2. https://www.dhl.com/global-en/home/press/press-archive/2018/rapid-response-from-the-air-medicines-successfully-delivered-using-a-parcel-drone-in-east-africa.html
3. https://newatlas.com/dhl-parcelcopter-africa/56663/
4. https://www.mckinsey.com/featured-insights/reimagining-mobility
5. https://www.mckinsey.com/featured-insights/reimagining-mobility

6. https://www.naco.org/resources/featured/connected-auto-nomous-vehicles-toolkit#:~:text=Connected%20and%20automated%20vehicles%20%28CAVs%29%20are%20two%20separate,is%20important%20to%20understand%20these%20distinctions%20and%20levels.

7. https://www.sae.org

8. https://www.autopilotreview.com/self-driving-cars-sae-levels/

9. https://www.cpuc.ca.gov/news-and-updates/all-news/cpuc-issues-first-driverless-autonomous-vehicle-passenger-service-deployment-permit

10. https://www.ga-asi.com/remotely-piloted-aircraft/predator-xp

11. https://www.inc.com/nick-hobson/elon-musk-says-hes-close-to-solving-one-of-hardest-technical-problems-thats-ever-existed-is-he-really.html

12. https://percepto.co/what-are-the-differences-bet-ween-uav-uas-and-autonomous-drones/

13. https://www.persistencemarketresearch.com/market-research/autonomous-underwater-vehicles-market.asp

14. https://www.britannica.com/biography/Montgolfier-brothers

15. https://www.teslasociety.com/radio.htm#:~:text=As%20early%20as%201892%2C%20Nikola,in%201898%2C%20Madison%20Square%20Garden

16. https://consortiq.com/drone-industry-outlook-us-2020-2030/

17. https://www.pwc.co.uk/services/sustainability-climate-change/insights/autonomous-electric-vehicles.html

18. https://static1.squarespace.com/static/585c3439be65942f022bb-f9b/t/591a2e4be6f2e1c13df930c5/1494888038959/RethinkX+Report_051517.pdf?pdf=RethinkingTransportation

19. https://linchpinseo.com/trends-shaping-the-ride-sharing-indus-try/

20. https://static1.squarespace.com/static/585c3439be65942f022bb-f9b/t/591a2e4be6f2e1c13df930c5/1494888038959/RethinkX+Report_051517.pdf?pdf=RethinkingTransportation

21. https://techcrunch.com/2021/05/24/light-is-the-key-to-long-ran-ge-fully-autonomous-evs/

22. https://www.morningstar.com/articles/1073357/is-teslas-disrup-tion-worth-the-price

23. https://www.pwc.co.uk/services/sustainability-climate-change/insights/autonomous-electric-vehicles.html

24. https://www.accenture.com/_acnmedia/pdf-60/accenture-insu-rance-autonomous-vehicles-pov.pdf

25. https://www.tesla.com

26. https://www.tesmanian.com/blogs/tesmanian-blog/tesla-evs-with-autonomous-driving-is-an-accelerant-to-sustainable-energy-which-is-a-fundamental-value-of-the-company

27. https://electrek.co/2022/10/20/tesla-progress-4680-batte-ry-cells-reduces-dependence/

28. https://www.tesmanian.com/blogs/tesmanian-blog/tesla-evs-with-autonomous-driving-is-an-accelerant-to-sustainable-energy-which-is-a-fundamental-value-of-the-company

29. https://companiesmarketcap.com/tesla/marketcap/

30. https://corporatefinanceinstitute.com/resources/knowledge/other/vehicle-to-everything-v2x/

31. https://www.weforum.org/agenda/2021/07/why-the-future-for-cars-is-connected/

32. https://www.marketsandmarkets.com/Market-Reports/unman-ned-aerial-vehicles-uav-market-662.html?gclid=EAIaIQobChMIv-qf71_jY8AIVBvfjBx3PCAIcEAAYAiAAEgLl0fD_BwE

33. https://droneii.com/product/drone-market-report-2020-2025

34. https://www.businesswire.com/news/home/20220907005787/en/Drone-ServicingRepair-Global-Market-Report-2022-Incre-asing-Applications-in-Precision-Farming-Fueling-Growth---Rese-archAndMarkets.com

35. https://www.alliedmarketresearch.com/underwater-drone-mar-ket-A08682

36. https://www.persistencemarketresearch.com/market-research/autonomous-underwater-vehicles-market.asp

37. https://www.verifiedmarketresearch.com/product/unman-ned-surface-vehicle-usv-market/

38. https://www.persistencemarketresearch.com/mediarelease/autonomous-underwater-vehicles-market.asp

39. https://www.databridgemarketresearch.com/reports/north-america-unmanned-surface-vehicle-usv-market

40. https://www.persistencemarketresearch.com/market-rese-arch/autonomous-underwater-vehicles-market.asp

11. https://vtechworks.lib.vt.edu/bitstream/handle/10919/100104/Effects%20of%20Drone%20Delivery%20US_September%202020.pdf?sequence=1&isAllowed=y

42. https://finance.yahoo.com/news/china-deliver-giant-meitu-an-raises-072519201.html

43. https://www.mckinsey.com/industries/automotive-and-assem-bly/our-insights/israel-hot-spot-for-future-mobility-technolo-gies#

44. https://www.mckinsey.com/industries/automotive-and-assem-bly/our-insights/can-the-automotive-industry-scale-fast-enough

45. https://www.mckinsey.com/industries/automotive-and-assem-bly/our-insights/start-me-up-where-mobility-investments-are-going

46. https://www.grandviewresearch.com/industry-analysis/glo-bal-commercial-drones-market#:~:text=The%20global%20commercial%20drone%20market%20size%20was%20va-lued,multiple%20applications%20ranging%20from%20filmma-king%20to%20emergency%20response.

47. https://www.alliedmarketresearch.com/autonomous-vehi-cle-market

48. https://www.alliedmarketresearch.com/underwater-dro-ne-market-A08682

49. https://avy.eu

50. https://enterprise-insights.dji.com/blog/let-drones-search-so-you-can-rescue-norway-landslide-m300

51. https://enterprise-insights.dji.com/blog/let-drones-search-so-you-can-rescue-norway-landslide-m300

52. https://www.weforum.org/agenda/2021/05/here-s-why-embra-cing-new-technologies-is-vital-for-haiti/

53. https://www.forbes.com/sites/bernardmarr/2020/07/17/5-ways-self-driving-cars-could-make-our-world-and-our-lives-better/?sh=3c5e838b42a3

54. https://www.nhtsa.gov/technology-innovation/automated-vehi-cles-safety

55. https://techxplore.com/news/2020-01-autonomous-vehi-cles-benefit-health-cars.html#:~:text=The%20use%20of%20autonomous%20vehicles%20is%20likely%20to,savings%20esti-mated%20at%20over%20%24200%20billion%20a%20year.

56. https://its.ucdavis.edu/research/publications/?frame=htt-ps%3A%2F%2Fitspubs.ucdavis.edu%2Findex.php%2Frese-arch%2Fpublications%2Fpublication-detail%2F%3Fpub_id%3D2723

57. https://techxplore.com/news/2020-01-autonomous-vehi-cles-benefit-health-cars.html#:~:text=The%20use%20of%20autonomous%20vehicles%20is%20likely%20to,savings%20esti-mated%20at%20over%20%24200%20billion%20a%20year.

58. https://uavcoach.com/drones-for-good/

59. https://www.sciencedaily.com/relea-ses/2020/11/201103112526.htm

60. https://droneseed.com

61. https://www.dronegenuity.com/ways-drones-help-save-the-environment/

62. https://www.sea-kit.com

63. https://www.auvsi.org/industry-news/fugro-sea-kit-develop-new-usvs-can-deploy-rovs-and-auvs-inspections

64. https://transmitter.ieee.org/auvs-how-autonomous-underwa-ter-vehicles-protect-oceans-and-divers/

65. https://reubenwu.com/home

66. https://dronedj.com/2020/03/16/matternet-new-drone-station-looks-great/
67. https://www.mckinsey.com/features/mckinsey-center-for-future-mobility/overview/autonomous-driving
68. https://www.skydio.com
69. https://www.forbes.com/sites/markminevich/2020/04/21/how-japan-is-tackling-the-national--global-infrastructure-crisis--pioneering-social-impact/?sh=e4396372eaf6
70. https://www.weforum.org/agenda/2021/08/how-drones-unlock-greener-infrastructure-inspection/
71. https://www.skydio.com/blog/jiw-grows-bridge-inspection-business-70x-by-switching-to-skydio
72. https://www.skydio.com/blog/jiw-grows-bridge-inspection-business-70x-by-switching-to-skydio/
73. https://www.forbes.com/sites/thomasbrewster/2021/03/01/self-flying-drone-startup-skydio-hits-1-billion-valuation-after-170-million-raise/?sh=c6ed9db7c813
74. https://sdg.iisd.org/commentary/guest-articles/drones-for-sdgs-fast-low-cost-delivery-of-health-care-supplies-for-remote-populations-in-malawi/
75. http://breakthrough.unglobalcompact.org
76. https://www.borgenmagazine.com/using-drones-to-combat-poverty/
77. https://css.umich.edu/factsheets/autonomous-vehicles-factsheet
78. https://vtechworks.lib.vt.edu/bitstream/handle/10919/100104/Effects%20of%20Drone%20Delivery%20US_September%202020.pdf?sequence=1&isAllowed=y
79. https://www.weforum.org/agenda/2015/06/how-to-use-drones-for-development/
80. http://css.umich.edu/factsheets/autonomous-vehicles-factsheet
81. https://mobilitylab.org/2016/06/16/two-keys-autonomous-vehicles-ease-congestion/
82. http://css.umich.edu/sites/default/files/Autonomous%20Vehicles_CSS16-18_e2020.pdf
83. https://www.weforum.org/agenda/2021/08/how-drones-unlock-greener-infrastructure-inspection/
84. https://www.automotive-iq.com/events-autonomousvehicles/blog/self-driving-sustainability
85. https://thecorrespondent.com/800/the-deep-seabed-holds-vast-knowledge-about-how-earth-works-thats-why-scientists-are-finally-mapping-the-ocean-floor/836671871200-483141ea#:~:text=Only%2020%25%20of%20the%20entire%20ocean%20floor%20of,or%20what%20kinds%20of%20organisms%20are%20living%20there.
86. https://www.saildrone.com/
87. https://www.blueyerobotics.com/products/pioneer
88. https://www.pwc.co.uk/sustainability-climate-change/assets/innovation-for-the-earth.pdf
89. https://hbr.org/2016/06/companies-are-turning-drones-into-a-competitive-advantage
90. https://www.forbes.com/sites/esri/2020/11/10/the-three-business-benefits-of-drones/?sh=6635225c2bf4
91. http://breakthrough.unglobalcompact.org/site/assets/files/1280/hhw-16-0014-d_n_uas.pdf
92. https://www.cbinsights.com/research/autonomous-driverless-vehicles-corporations-list/
93. https://www.accenture.com/_acnmedia/pdf-60/accenture-insurance-autonomous-vehicles-pov.pdf
94. https://www.accenture.com/_acnmedia/pdf-60/accenture-insurance-autonomous-vehicles-pov.pdf
95. https://data.worldbank.org/indicator/SP.RUR.TOTL.ZS?end=2018&start=1960&view=chart
96. https://www.weforum.org/agenda/2020/04/medicines-from-the-sky-how-a-drone-may-save-your-life/
97. https://www.dronesinhealthcare.com/
98. https://www.dronesinhealthcare.com/
99. https://healthtechmagazine.net/article/2020/12/what-know-about-autonomous-vehicles-healthcare
100. https://avy.eu/stories/drones-for-health-project/
101. https://coldchain-tech.com/
102. https://mttr.net/
103. https://flyzipline.com
104. https://mttr.net/images/Matternet.New_Station_Unveil.2020.03.10.pdf
105. https://about.ups.com/us/en/newsroom/press-releases/innovation-driven/ups-flight-forward-cvs-to-launch-residential-drone-delivery-service-in-florida-retirement-community-to-assist-in-coronavirus-response.html
106. https://uavcoach.com/drones-for-good/
107. https://www.gamaya.com/
108. https://delair.aero/
109. https://www.eu-startups.com/2020/11/how-are-drones-are-changing-the-face-of-agriculture/
110. https://www.flyzipline.com
111. https://flyzipline.com/live/
112. https://www.cnbc.com/2020/06/16/zipline-disruptor-50.html
113. https://www.cmaj.ca/content/190/3/E88
114. https://www.xa.com/en
115. https://www.xa.com/en/p100
116. www.xa.com/en/news/official/xag/69
117. https://borgenproject.org/drones-in-china/
118. https://news.cgtn.com/news/2020-10-02/Agricultural-productivity-flies-high-with-drones-in-poverty-hit-areas-UgaQ3MXWhO/index.html
119. https://asiatimes.com/2020/10/china-experiencing-a-drone-revolution-in-agriculture/
120. http://www.fao.org/3/I8494EN/i8494en.pdf
121. https://19january2017snapshot.epa.gov/climate-impacts/climate-impacts-agriculture-and-food-supply_.html#:~:text=Many%20weeds%2C%20pests%2C%20and%20fungi%20thrive%20under%20warmer,pests%20are%20likely%20to%20increase%20with%20climate%20change.
122. https://www.un.org/development/desa/en/news/population/world-population-prospects-2019.html
123. https://www.nhtsa.gov/technology-innovation/automated-vehicles-safety
124. https://www.mckinsey.com/industries/automotive-and-assembly/our-insights/mapping-the-automotive-software-and-electronics-landscape-through-2030
125. https://www.nhtsa.gov/technology-innovation/automated-vehicles-safety
126. https://cece.vt.edu/content/dam/econdev_vt_edu/projects/technology/Virginia%20Tech%20%20Measuring%20the%20Effects%20of%20Drone%20Delivery%20in%20the%20United%20States_September%202020.pdf
127. https://www.issaerospace.com/uav-sectors/energy-sector/
128. https://www.chooseenergy.com/news/article/drones-used-energy-sector/
129. https://www.hoversurf.com
130. https://droneii.com/uam-urban-air-mobility
131. https://www.hoversurf.com/business-1
132. https://www.nando-drone.com
133. https://itrade.gov.il/philippines/2021/05/19/israels-drones-set-to-improve-civilian-life/
134. https://www.issaerospace.com/about-us/
135. https://www.grandviewresearch.com/industry-analysis/autonomous-vehicles-market
136. https://phys.org/news/2018-02-maximizing-environmental-benefits-autonomous-vehicles.html
137. https://techcrunch.com/2021/05/24/light-is-the-key-to-long-range-fully-autonomous-evs/
138. https://www.tdworld.com/grid-innovations/generation-and-renewables/article/21122677/drones-aid-in-remote-monitoring-of-power-plant-assets
139. https://www.energy.gov/sites/prod/files/2021/01/f82/us-hydropower-market-report-full-2021.pdf

140. https://3dinsider.com/drone-business-opportunities/#:~:text=Underwater%20drones%20can%20be%20used%20to%20conduct%20marine,or%20you%20can%20rent%20out%20underwater%20drone%20equipment.
141. https://seabed2030.org/
142. https://www.alliedmarketresearch.com/underwater-drone-market-A09682
143. https://sendronenews.com/submersible-underwater-drones-business-opportunities/
144. https://sendronenews.com/submersible-underwater-drones-business-opportunities/
145. https://seabed2030.org
146. https://www.hydro-international.com/content/article/who-is-going-to-map-the-high-seas#_edn1
147. https://www.globenewswire.com/news-release/2021/07/15/2263189/0/en/Underwater-Drone-Market-Value-Predicted-To-Reach-US-7-500-2-Million-By-2028-Covering-COVID-19-Impact-Acumen-Research-and-Consulting.html
148. https://www.saildrone.com
149. https://www.hydro-international.com/content/article/who-is-going-to-map-the-high-seas#_edn1
150. https://www.saildrone.com/solutions/ocean-mapping
151. https://unintendedconsequenc.es/autonomous-vehicles-scaling-risk/
152. https://knowledge.wharton.upenn.edu/article/driverless-cars-pros-and-cons/
153. https://www.weforum.org/agenda/2019/07/self-driving-cars-downsides/
154. https://web.mit.edu/12.000/www/m2016/finalwebsite/problems/humanrights.html
155. https://www.nytimes.com/2019/11/03/us/drones-crime.html
156. https://grinddrone.com/drone-features/advantages-and-disadvantages-drone

Chapter 8: Blockchain

1. https://doi.org/10.1201/9780429283987
2. https://www.mordorintelligence.com/industry-reports/cotton-market
3. https://www.wto.org/english/res_e/reser_e/workshop_blockchain_21219_e.htm
4. https://www.nagarro.com/en/blog/blockchain-organic-cotton-traceability
5. https://crosstextiles.com/news/detail/33/?title=cross-textiles-is-leading-the-industry-with-its-sustainable-practices
6. https://sourcingjournal.com/topics/raw-materials/aware-fully-traceable-recycled-cotton-fibers-fabrics-blockchain-startup-dutch-223290/
7. https://calikdenim.com
8. https://www.fibre2fashion.com/news/textile-news/dutch-startup-the-movement-completes-1-million-pre-seed-round-279534-newsdetails.htm
9. https://digital-strategy.ec.europa.eu/en/policies/blockchain-strategy
10. https://www.mckinsey.com/business-functions/mckinsey-digital/our-insights/blockchain-beyond-the-hype-what-is-the-strategic-business-value
11. https://www.enisa.europa.eu/topics/csirts-in-europe/glossary/blockchain
12. https://www3.weforum.org/docs/WEF_Building-Blockchains.pdf
13. https://www.accenture.com/_acnmedia/pdf-68/accenture-808045-blockchainpov-rgb.pdf
14. https://innovation.wfp.org/project/building-blocks
15. https://innovation.wfp.org/project/building-blocks
16. https://www.sciencedirect.com/science/article/pii/S1877050919310178
17. https://www.blockchain-council.org/blockchain/a-detailed-history-of-blockchain-from-the-establishment-to-broad-adoption/
18. https://satoshi.nakamotoinstitute.org
19. https://www.blockchain-council.org/blockchain/a-detailed-history-of-blockchain-from-the-establishment-to-broad-adoption/
20. https://ycharts.com/indicators/bitcoin_blockchain_size
21. https://ethereum.org/en/
22. https://www3.weforum.org/docs/WEF_Building-Blockchains.pdf
23. https://www.blockchain-council.org/blockchain/a-detailed-history-of-blockchain-from-the-establishment-to-broad-adoption/
24. https://time.com/nextadvisor/investing/cryptocurrency/bitcoin-price-history/
25. https://sectigostore.com/blog/what-is-crypto-mining-how-cryptocurrency-mining-works/
26. https://home.treasury.gov/system/files/136/CryptoAsset_EO5.pdf
27. https://fortunly.com/statistics/blockchain-statistics/#gref
28. https://www.hyperledger.org/learn/publications/walmart-case-study
29. https://www.exporis.ch/articles/customer-experience-in-banking-to-drive-revenue/
30. https://developer.cisco.com/blockchain
31. https://www.fortunebusinessinsights.com/industry-reports/blockchain-market-100072
32. https://nowpayments.io/blog/blockchain-as-a-service
33. https://nowpayments.io/blog/blockchain-as-a-service
34. https://www.gsb.stanford.edu/sites/gsb/files/publication-pdf/study-blockchain-impact-moving-beyond-hype.pdf
35. https://ihodl.com/topnews/2021-07-23/blockchain-startups-raised-44b-q2-cb-insights/
36. https://www.cbinsights.com/research/blockchain-vc-ico-funding/
37. https://www.nytimes.com/2021/12/01/business/dealbook/crypto-venture-capital.html
38. https://www.reportlinker.com/p05987968/Blockchain-AI-Market-by-Technology-Component-Deployment-Mode-Organization-Size-Application-Vertical-And-Region-Global-Forecast-to.html?utm_source=GNW
39. https://www.gsb.stanford.edu/sites/gsb/files/publication-pdf/study-blockchain-impact-moving-beyond-hype.pdf
40. https://www.fmiblog.com/2022/03/11/blockchain-technology-market-research-report-2022-global-forecast-till-2030/
41. https://consensys.net/blockchain-use-cases/global-trade-and-commerce/
42. https://www.cnbc.com/advertorial/global-trade-now-faces-a-us3point4-trillion-financing-gap/
43. https://fortunly.com/statistics/blockchain-statistics/
44. https://webinarcare.com/best-blockchain-as-a-service-providers/blockchain-as-a-service-providers-statistics/#0
45. https://www.marketsandmarkets.com/Market-Reports/blockchain-technology-market-90100890.html#:~:text=%5B441%20Pages%20Report%5D%20The%20Blockchain,68.4%25%20during%20the%20forecast%20period.
46. https://www.marketsandmarkets.com/Market-Reports/crypto-currency-market-158061641.html
47. https://www.reportlinker.com/p05987968/Blockchain-AI-Market-by-Technology-Component-Deployment-Mode-Organization-Size-Application-Vertical-And-Region-Global-Forecast-to.html?utm_source=GNW
48. https://www.accenture.com/_acnmedia/pdf-68/accenture-808045-blockchainpov-rgb.pdf
49. https://www.fao.org/in-action/pig-farmers-in-papua-new-guinea/en/

50. https://www.forbes.com/sites/darrynpollock/2020/02/27/block-chain-for-good-how-the-united-nations-is-looking-to-leverage-technology/?sh=18d8d1c2543d

51. https://www.jbs.cam.ac.uk/wp-content/uploads/2020/08/2019-09-ccaf-2nd-global-cryptoasset-benchmarking.pdf

52. https://www.ibm.com/case-studies/energy-blockchain-labs-inc

53. https://mediacenter.ibm.com/media/Energy+Blockchain+Labs+A+facilitating+carbon+reduction+with+IBM+Blockchain/1_j1cot0z5

54. Note; PoW refers to the decentralized system that powers the Bitcoin network, with the model requiring huge amounts of energy to validate transactions and mint new tokens; but PoS allows miners to mine and validate block transactions based on the number of coins they hold.

55. https://www.bitget.com/academy/en/article-details/What-is-the-PoS-and-How-is-it-different-from-PoW

56. https://www.undp.org/content/undp/en/home/blog/2017/7/13/What-kind-of-blender-do-we-need-to-finance-the-SDGs-.html

57. https://doi.org/10.1016/j.rser.2020.109949

58. https://www.sustainability-times.com/sustainable-business/block-chain-can-be-a-vital-tool-to-boost-sustainability/

59. https://www.memphis.edu/mediaroom/releases/2019/july/reme-dichain.php

60. https://www.remedichain.org

61. https://www.forbes.com/sites/forbestechcouncil/2020/01/13/the-circular-economy-and-sustainability-powered-by-block-chain/?sh=51e2b8f3b8cff

62. https://www.provenance.org

63. https://www.provenance.org/news-insights/provenan-ce-wins-1-million-euro-prize-from-the-european-commissi-on-for-blockchains-for-social-good

64. https://www.provenance.org/whitepaper

65. https://www.businesswire.com/news/home/20210519005633/en/Provenance-Launches-New-Public-Decentralized-Block-chain-for-Financial-Services

66. https://www.mckinsey.com/featured-insights/employ-ment-and-growth/how-digital-finance-could-boost-growth-in-emerging-economies

67. https://www.mckinsey.com/featured-insights/employ-ment-and-growth/how-digital-finance-could-boost-growth-in-emerging-economies

68. https://www.gatesfoundation.org/Ideas/Media-Center/Press-Releases/2017/10/Bill-Melinda-Gates-Foundation-Relea-ses-Open-Source-Software-to-Expand-Access-to-Financial-Ser-vices

69. https://twitter.com/UtilityTheory/status/1468645983059947522

70. https://www.cgdev.org/blog/migrant-remittances-will-plum-met-here-what-means-global-development

71. https://uploads-ssl.webflow.com/601814030e1e39d44b52570b/60da59be8d5d5b4fbc1f7165_Blockchain%20&%20the%20SDGs-How%20Decentralisation%20Can%20Make%20a%20Difference.pdf

72. https://www.stellar.org

73. https://blogs.worldbank.org/peoplemove/data-release-remit-tances-low-and-middle-income-countries-track-reach-551-bil-lion-2019

74. https://cardanocataly.st/

75. https://cardano.org

76. https://theconversation.com/ethiopias-blockchain-deal-is-a-watershed-moment-for-the-technology-and-for-africa-160719#:%7E:text=In%20April%20the%20Ethiopian%20gover-nment%20confirmed%20that%20it,which%20will%20be%20used%20to%20store%20educational%20records.

77. https://ambcrypto.com/cardanos-slow-and-steady-project-cata-lyst-now-holds-more-than-1b/

78. https://uploads-ssl.webflow.com/601814030e1e39d44b-52570b/60da59be8d5d5b4fbc1f7165_Blockchain%20&%20the%20SDGs-How%20Decentralisation%20Can%20Make%20a%20Difference.pdf

79. https://documents1.worldbank.org/curated/en/187761468179367706/pdf/WPS7255.pdf#page=3

80. https://www.dw.com/en/blockchain-the-future-for-remittan-ce-payments/a-42375862

81. https://innovecs.com/blog/blockchain-in-healthcare/

82. https://talentsprint.com/blog/xp/how-blockchain-enabled-asli-medicine-became-the-perfect-solution-to-eliminate-fake-me-dicine/

83. https://timestech.in/blockchain-in-education-sec-tor-the-next-revolution/

84. https://www.socialalphafoundation.org

85. https://medium.com/@SocialAlpha/social-alpha-block-chain-for-social-impact-hackathon-42802909f016

86. https://bitcoinafrica.io/2018/04/17/the-sun-exchange-launches-sunex-token-to-fund-its-solar-project-insurance-fund/

87. https://blockchainmagazine.net/russias-natio-nal-energy-grid-operator-to-test-blockchain-in-retail-sector/

88. https://itsblockchain.com/top-5-cryptocurrency-pro-jects-in-supply-chain/

89. https://win.systems/wp-content/uploads/2018/09/block-chain-for-humanity-1.pdf

90. https://www.worldbank.org/en/news/feature/2020/03/23/glo-bal-public-procurement-database-share-compare-improve

91. https://www3.weforum.org/docs/WEF_Blockchain_Govern-ment_Transparency_Report.pdf

92. https://modex.tech/blockchain-the-solution-for-public-procu-rement-corruption/

93. https://hbr.org/2017/01/the-truth-about-blockchain

94. https://vaultsecurity.io/category/the-future-of-blockchain-tech-nology

95. https://www2.deloitte.com/us/en/pages/energy-and-resources/articles/blockchain-use-cases-energy-resources-industry-dis-ruptor.html

96. https://globalblockchainsummit.com/benefits/

97. https://www.forbes.com/sites/alexknapp/2019/03/04/this-blockchain-startup-is-partnering-with-fashion-giants-to-make-organic-cotton-traceable/?sh=458939e61fd2

98. https://www.information-age.com/five-blockchain-use-ca-ses-123484558/

99. https://www.cut.eco/find-out-more

100. https://doi.org/10.1016/j.cities.2021.103325

101. https://uploads-ssl.webflow.com/601814030e1e39d44b-52570b/60da59be8d5d5b4fbc1f7165_Blockchain%20&%20the%20SDGs-How%20Decentralisation%20Can%20Make%20a%20Difference.pdf

102. https://www.accenture.com/_acnmedia/PDF-93/Accentu-re-Tracing-Supply-Chain-Blockchain-Study-PoV.pdf#zoom=50

103. https://www.bext360.com

104. https://www.forbes.com/sites/alexknapp/2019/03/04/this-blockchain-startup-is-partnering-with-fashion-giants-to-make-organic-cotton-traceable/?sh=458939e61fd2

105. https://fashionforgood.com/our_news/successfully-tra-cing-organic-cotton-with-innovative-technologies/#:%7E:tex-t=The%20Organic%20Cotton%20Traceability%20Pilot%20was%20initiated%20in,to%20in-field%20testing%20which%20concluded%20this%20past%20summer

106. https://doi.org/10.3389/fbloc.2020.00007

107. https://etherisc.com

108. https://www.asiablockchainreview.com/xox-partners-ant-chain-to-enhance-food-traceability/#:%7E:text=AntChain%20TaaS%20is%20a%20blockchain-based%20traceability%20solution%20combined,end-to-end%20transparency%20on%20information%20along%20the%20supply%20chain

109. https://restofworld.org/2020/ant-group-financial-empire/
110. https://www.irena.org/newsroom/articles/2018/Nov/Block-chain-Enabling-The-Internet-of-Electricity
111. https://www.reutersevents.com/sustainability/cookstoves-car-bon-markets-how-blockchain-supercharging-sustainability
112. https://www.agridigital.io
113. https://www.agridigital.io/reports/case-study-itochu-australia
114. https://www.weforum.org/project/building-blocks
115. https://www.weforum.org/agenda/2021/06/blockchain-can-help-us-beat-climate-change-heres-how/
116. https://www.brooklyn.energy/about
117. https://unfccc.int/process-and-meetings/the-paris-agreement/nationally-determined-contributions-ndcs/nationally-determin-ed-contributions-ndcs
118. https://www.genesis-mining.com/
119. https://www.iea.org/reports/sdg7-data-and-projections/ac-cess-to-electricity
120. https://www.impactppa.com/wp-content/uploads/2018/03/Im-pactPPA_WP_v1.2WEB.pdf
121. https://www.brooklyn.energy/about
122. https://www.cleantech.com/from-the-brooklyn-microgrid-to-exergy-a-conversation-with-lawrence-orsini-ceo-of-lo3-energy/
123. https://www.energyweb.org
124. https://rowanenergy.com
125. https://gtime.io/tecnologia/
126. https://www.powerchain.energy
127. https://www.besc.online/consortium
128. https://www2.deloitte.com/us/en/pages/public-sector/articles/blockchain-opportunities-for-health-care.html
129. https://www.bitcoininsider.org/article/93424/healthcare-ma-kes-case-blockchain-use-despite-challenges
130. https://theblockbox.io/blog/blockchain-technology-in-healthca-re-in-2021/
131. https://theblockbox.io/blog/blockchain-technology-in-healthca-re-in-2021/
132. https://builtin.com/blockchain/blockchain-healthcare-applicati-ons-companies
133. https://www.koibanx.com
134. https://aithority.com/technology/blockchain/colombian-govern-ment-selects-vitalpass-co-created-by-auna-ideas-and-built-on-al-gorand-blockchain-as-the-nations-official-digital-vaccinati-on-passport/
135. https://emergingmarkets.today/colombia-launches-first-block-chain-based-system-to-track-covid-19-vaccination/
136. https://www.coindesk.com/business/2022/08/18/blockchain-pro-tocol-algorand-leads-22m-investment-round-in-tokenizati-on-firm-koibanx/
137. https://www.unicef.org/innovation/fundgraduate/StaTwig
138. https://www.bbc.com/news/technology-56012952
139. https://www.weforum.org/agenda/2020/09/3-ways-block-chain-can-contribute-to-sustainable-development/
140. https://openledger.info/insights/blockchain-law-regulati-ons/#:~:text=A%20multitude%20of%20countries%20world-wide%2C%20including%20the%20United,indirect%20and%-2For%20direct%20tactics%20to%20regulate%20the%20industry.

Chapter 9: SpaceTech

1. https://www.jpl.nasa.gov/missions/gravity-recovery-and-clim-te-experiment-grace
2. https://africanews.space/leveraging-space-technologies-to-achie-ve-sdg-6-clean-water-and-sanitation
3. https://www.afdb.org/en/documents/water-strate-gy-2021-2025-towards-water-secure-africa
4. https://africanews.space/leveraging-space-technologies-to-achie-ve-sdg-6-clean-water-and-sanitation/
5. https://www.pwc.fr/en/industrie/secteur-spatial/pwc-space-team-public-reports-and-articles/main-trends-and-challenges-in-the-space-sector.html
6. https://www.feedough.com/what-is-space-tech/
7. https://www.perkinscoie.com/images/content/2/5/250570/10-ETT-Chapter-10-Spacetech.pdf
8. https://www.frontiersin.org/articles/10.3389/frspt.2020.00001/full#B18
9. https://solarsystem.nasa.gov/basics/chapter9-1/
10. https://www.nasa.gov/centers/ames/partnerships/spinoff.html
11. https://www.nasa.gov/centers/ames/partnerships/spinoff.html
12. https://www.ucsusa.org/resources/satellite-database
13. https://www.geospatialworld.net/blogs/how-many-satellites-are-orbiting-the-earth-in-2021/
14. https://www.ucsusa.org/resources/satellite-database
15. https://www.geospatialworld.net/prime/how-many-satelli-tes-orbiting
16. https://www.esa.int/Enabling_Support/Operations/ESA_Ground_Stations/Estrack_ground_stations
17. https://www.esa.int/Enabling_Support/Operations/ESA_Ground_Stations/Estrack_ground_stations
18. https://www.esa.int/Enabling_Support/Operations/ESA_Ground_Stations/Estrack_ground_stations
19. https://www.jpl.nasa.gov
20. https://doi.org/10.3844/jastsp.2017.1.8
21. https://www.spacex.com
22. https://provscons.com/heres-why-spacex-uses-kerosene/
23. https://www.fastcompany.com/90724476/most-innova-tive-companies-space-2022
24. https://www.forbes.com/sites/alexkonrad/2022/08/11/austra-lian-south-korean-investors-pour-more-cash into-spacex-at-125-billion/?sh=627a7d764163
25. https://www.maxar.com
26. https://www.sciencedirect.com/science/article/abs/pii/S009457651200197X?via%3Dihub
27. https://www.nasa.gov/center/armstrong/features/space-tech-for-suborbital-flight.html
28. https://www.nasa.gov/directorates/spacetech/flightopportuni-ties/index.html
29. https://www3.weforum.org/docs/WEF_GFC_Six_ways_space_technologies_2020.pdf
30. https://www3.weforum.org/docs/WEF_GFC_Six_ways_space_technologies_2020.pdf
31. https://www.researchandmarkets.com/reports/5574887/global-space-economy-market-analysis-byclient?utm_source=-CI&utm_medium=PressRelease&utm_code=s235sd&utm_campaign=1687137+-+Global+%24540%2b+Billion+S-pace+Economy+Markets+to+2026&utm_exec=chdo54prd
32. https://www.investopedia.com/space-economy-seen-near-ly-usd178-billion-in-investments-since-2011- 5113282
33. https://www.cnbc.com/2022/01/18/space-investing-q4-report-companies-hit-record-14point5-billion-in 2021.html
34. https://www.spacecapital.com/quarterly
35. https://www.prnewswire.com/news-releases/global-space-sys-tems-satellites--launchers-market-research report-2021-to-2026---by-payload-platform-service-type-vehicle-type-orbit-type-end-user-and-region 301455480.html
36. https://www.morganstanley.com/ideas/investing-in-space
37. https://www.mckinsey.com/industries/aerospace-and-defense/our-insights/a-different-space-race-raising capital-and-accelera-ting-growth-in-space
38. https://www.spacetech.global/spacetech-industry-in-figures
39. https://www.nsr.com/nsr-in-orbit-servicing-space-situatio-nal-awareness-market-forecast-to-generate-6-2-b in-the-next-decade/

40. https://www.nsr.com/nsr-in-orbit-servicing-space-situatio-nal-awareness-market-forecast-to-generate-6-2-b in-the-next-decade/
41. https://idstch.com/space/global-space-propulsion-market/
42. https://www.uschamber.com/space/space-economy-4-trends-to-watch-in-2022
43. https://www.spacetech.global/spacetech-industry-in-figu-res#:~:text=Valued%20at%20%244.75B%2C%20the,air%20transportation%2C%20and%20aerospace%20Internet.
44. https://www.nsr.com/onenewspage-nsr-report-in-orbit-satelli-te-servicing-and-space-situational-awareness-iosm4-opportu-nity/
45. https://www.mckinsey.com/industries/aerospace-and-defense/our-insights/how-will-the-space-economy-change-the-world
46. https://www.spacetech.global
47. https://analytics.dkv.global/spacetech/Publicly-Traded-Compa-nies-in-Space=
48. Tech-Industry-2021-Report.pdf
49. https://sustainabledevelopment.un.org/post2015/transfor-mingourworld/publication
50. https://sustainableearth.biomedcentral.com/articles/10.1186/s42055-021-00045-6
51. https://www.morganstanley.com/ideas/space-earth-sustainability
52. https://www3.weforum.org/docs/WEF_GFC_Six_ways_space_technologies_2020.pdf
53. https://www.inmarsat.com/en/index.html
54. https://unctad.org/system/files/official-document/ecn162020d3_en.pdf
55. https://www.opendatacube.org
56. https://www.unoosa.org/oosa/en/ourwork/space4sdgs/sdg2.html
57. https://www.weo-water.com/sustainable-agriculture/
58. https://www.pixxel.space
59. https://www.financialexpress.com/defence/space-startup-pixxel-reaches-for-the-sky-plans-six-earth-imaging-satelli-tes-in-2023/2658547/
60. https://unctad.org/system/files/official-document/ecn162020d3_en.pdf
61. https://www.ncbi.nlm.nih.gov/pmc/articles/PMC3154638/
62. https://varda.com
63. https://www.spaceforge.co.uk
64. https://earlymetrics.com/how-spacetech-startups-shape-futu-re-of-healthcare/
65. https://www.unoosa.org/oosa/en/ourwork/topics/spaceforwo-men/index.html
66. https://africanews.space/afas-establishes-african-network-wo-men-astronomy/
67. https://www.anza.holdings
68. https://africanews.space/2020-in-review-anza-capital/
69. https://space4water.org/news/unoosa-and-prince-sultan-bin-ab-dulaziz-international-prize-water-reinforce their-cooperation
70. https://africanews.space/leveraging-space-technologies-to-achie-ve-sdg-6-clean-water-and-sanitation/
71. https://pale-blue.co.jp/product/
72. https://www.unoosa.org/oosa/en/ourwork/space4sdgs/sdg7.html
73. https://www3.weforum.org/docs/WEF_GFC_Six_ways_space_technologies_2020.pdf
74. https://www.solstorm.io
75. https://www.solstorm.io/t
76. https://www.unoosa.org/oosa/en/ourwork/space4sdgs/sdg9.html
77. https://www3.weforum.org/docs/WEF_GFC_Six_ways_space_technologies_2020.pdf
78. https://www3.weforum.org/docs/WEF_GFC_Six_ways_space_technologies_2020.pdf
79. https://www.leviathanspace.com
80. https://www3.weforum.org/docs/WEF_GFC_Six_ways_space_technologies_2020.pdf
81. https://digitalurban.place
82. https://www.ukri.org/what-we-offer/supporting-innovation/innovation-stfc/business-incubation-centres/
83. https://www.ukri.org/news/satellite-technology-takes-ur-ban-planning-to-a-new-level/
84. https://digitalcommons.usu.edu/smallsat/2018/all2018/437/
85. https://www.unoosa.org/oosa/en/ourwork/space4sdgs/sdg12.html
86. https://www3.weforum.org/docs/WEF_GFC_Six_ways_space_technologies_2020.pdf
87. https://heo-robotics.com
88. https://totum.global
89. https://www.unoosa.org/oosa/en/ourwork/space4sdgs/sdg13.html
90. https://www.weforum.org/agenda/2021/03/space-techno-logy-tackle-climate-change/
91. https://www.ghgsat.com/en/
92. https://www.fastcompany.com/90724476/most-innova-tive-companies-space-2022
93. https://www.weforum.org/agenda/2021/03/space-techno-logy-tackle-climate-change/
94. https://www.unoosa.org/oosa/en/ourwork/space4sdgs/sdg14.html
95. https://www3.weforum.org/docs/WEF_GFC_Six_ways_space_technologies_2020.pdf
96. https://starboard.nz
97. https://fiskerforum.com/nz-space-tech-startup-helps-tackle-iuu-fishing/
98. https://www.nasa.gov/sites/default/files/files/Benefits-Stem-ming-from-Space-Exploration 2013-TAGGED.pdf
99. http://www.spaceref.com/news/viewsr.html?pid=19999;
100. https://www.perkinscoie.com/images/content/2/5/250570/10-ETT-Chapter-10-Spacetech.pdf
101. https://www.kiplinger.com/investing/etfs/602520/space-etfs
102. https://www.businessinsider.com/musk-highly-confident-spacex-will-send-humans-to-mars-2026-2020-12
103. https://speqtral.space
104. https://en.prnasia.com/releases/apac/speqtral-announces-spe-qtral-1-quantum-satellite-mission-for-ultra secure-communica-tions-350930.shtml
105. https://www.startus-insights.com/innovators-guide/top-10-spacetech-trends-innovations-2021/
106. https://spacetech.business
107. https://www.businessinsider.com/musk-highly-confident-spacex-will-send-humans-to-mars-2026-2020-12
108. https://www.nasa.gov/feature/goddard/2018/nasa-indus-try-team-creates-and-demonstrates-first quantum-sen-sor-for-satellite-gravimetry
109. https://www.sciencedirect.com/science/article/pii/S0370157321004142
110. https://www.analyticsinsight.net/how-microsoft-and-nasa-part-nership-is-taking-a-new-shape-in-spacetech/
111. https://analytics.dkv.global/spacetech/blockchain_in_space_q4_2021_onepager.pdf
112. https://www.spacefocus.com/space/nasa-lunar-gateway/
113. https://xyo.network
114. https://xylabs.com
115. https://xylabs.com/products/coin
116. https://www.geospatialworld.net/prime/building-the-wor-lds-first-blockchain-geospatial-network-backed with-crypto-graphy/
117. https://www.here.com
118. https://www.space.com/northrop-grumman-mev-2-docks-in-telsat-satellite
119. https://news.satnews.com/2021/05/25/astrosca-le-will-work-with-oneweb-to-develop-space-debris remova-val-innovations/

120. https://www.climate-kic.org/opinion/how-can-we-leverage-space-innovation-to-take-climate-action-on earth/
121. https://www3.weforum.org/docs/WEF_GFC_Six_ways_space_technologies_2020.pdf
122. https://www.iea.org/news/tackling-methane-emissions from-fossil-fuel-operations-is-essential-to-combat near-term-global warming
123. https://alen.space
124. https://alen.space/case-studies-nanosatellites/
125. https://www.dawnaerospace.com
126. https://www.methansat.org/?conversion_pg=www.edf.org%2Fclimate%2Fspace-technology-can-cut climate-pollution-earth
127. https://www.edf.org/climate/space-technology-can-cut-climate-pollution-earth
128. https://www.iea.org/news/tackling-methane-emissions-from-fossil-fuel-operations-is-essential-to-combat near-term-global-warming
129. https://www.copernicus.eu/en/about-copernicus
130. https://www.space4good.com/portfolio
131. https://sentinel.esa.int/web/sentinel/missions/sentinel-5p
132. https://www.morganstanley.com/ideas/space-earthsustainability#:~:text="A%20United%20Nations%20study%20found%20that%2052%25%20of,a%202.5%25%20difference%20in%20a%20country's%20GDP.%201
133. https://www.broadbandcommission.org/Documents/reports/bb-annualreport2015.pdf
134. https://www.icann.org/en/system/files/files/bcg-internet-economy-27jan14-en.pdf
135. https://www.broadbandcommission.org/Documents/reports/bb-annualreport2015.pdf
136. https://kleos.space
137. https://space-agency.public.lu/en/expertise/space-directory/kleos.html
138. https://g8c.com/wp-content/uploads/2021/07/White-Paper-Dawn-of-Aerospace-July-2021.pdf
139. https://www.satellitetoday.com/innovation/2017/10/12/satellite-launches-increase-threefold-next-decade/
140. https://www.ucsusa.org/resources/satellite-database#.XA1a6m-hKg2w https://www.cognitivespace.com
141. https://www.spaceflightinsider.com/organizations/bigelow-aerospace/bigelow-aerospace-spawns-spinoff company-to-market-its-space-stations/
142. https://bigelowaerospace.com
143. https://www.nasa.gov/content/bigelow-expandable-activity-module
144. https://www.bigelowspaceops.com
145. https://www.spaceflightinsider.com/organizations/bigelow-aerospace/bigelow-aerospace-spawns-spinoff company-to-market-its-space-stations/
146. https://www.esa.int/Safety_Security/Space_Debris/Space_debris_by_the_numbers
147. https://etpack.eu/the-space-debris-problem/
148. https://www.esa.int/Safety_Security/Space_Debris/Space_debris_by_the_numbers
149. https://www.weforum.org/agenda/2018/04/we-have-a-space-debris-problem-heres-how-to-solve-it/
150. https://orbitguardians.com/our-work
151. https://www.fortunebusinessinsights.com/space-debris-monitoring-and-removal-market-104070
152. https://www.weforum.org/agenda/2021/11/space-debris-satellite-international-space-station/
153. https://okapiorbits.space/satellite-operator-services/
154. https://sustainableearth.biomedcentral.com/track/pdf/10.1186/s42055-021-00045-6.pdf
155. https://astroscale.com
156. https://spacenews.com/uk-shortlists-astroscale-and-clears-space-for-multi-debris-removal-mission/
157. https://spacewatch.global/2021/11/astroscale-raises-109-million-on-bringing-total-to-300-million/
158. https://hummingbirdtech.com
159. https://www.basf.com/global/en/who-we-are/organization/group-companies/BASF_Venture Capital/portfolio/hummingbird.html
160. http://www.spacestepedu.com
161. https://www.climate-kic.org
162. http://www.g4geo.eu
163. https://www.feedough.com/what-is-space-tech

Chapter 10: Scaling Tech for Good

1. http://www.sparc-website.org
2. https://www.ncbi.nlm.nih.gov/pmc/articles/PMC9096635/
3. https://www.newfoodmagazine.com/article/160523/micro-bubble-fish-farming
4. https://futurism.com/neoscope/personalized-medicine-may-do-more-to-treat-rather-than-prevent-chronic-diseases
5. https://www3.weforum.org/docs/Unlocking_Technology_for_the_Global_Goals.pdf
6. https://www.futurefarming.com/Smart-farmers/Articles/2018/9/Microsoft-Great-potential-for-AI-in-agriculture-331961E/
7. https://www.mic.com/articles/48705/6-incredible-technologies-no-one-knows-about
8. https://www.weforum.org/agenda/2022/01/tech-trends-in-2022/
9. https://www.techforlife.net/our-book/
10. https://www3.weforum.org/docs/Unlocking_Technology_for_the_Global_Goals.pdf
11. https://stepupdeclaration.org/thecoalition
12. https://initiatives.weforum.org/2030vision-network/home
13. https://cybertechaccord.org
14. https://partnershiponai.org
15. https://www.jfklibrary.org/learn/about-jfk/historic-speeches/address-at-rice-university-on-the-nations-space-effort
16. https://www.techtarget.com/whatis/definition/moonshot
17. https://x.company/
18. https://www.microsoft.com/en-us/corporate-responsibility/sustainability/carbon-removal-program
19. https://www.bloomberg.com/news/articles/2022-05-03/elon-musk-alphabet-invest-in-carbon-removal-technology?leadSource=uverify%20wall
20. https://www.firstinsight.com/white-papers-posts/gen-z-shoppers-demand-sustainability
21. https://www.dosomething.org/us/collections/corona-virus-campaigns
22. https://www.voguebusiness.com/consumers/marketing-to-gen-z-during-covid-19
23. https://moonshotpirates.com/blog/how-gen-z-is-shaping-the-future-of-business/
24. https://www.usatoday.com/story/news/nation/2020/08/18/generation-z-may-most-creative-yet-study-says/5589601002/
25. https://www.fastcompany.com/90743143/gen-z-is-going-to-reinvent-the-supply-chain
26. https://www.usatoday.com/story/news/nation/2020/08/18/generation-z-may-most-creative-yet-study-says/5589601002/
27. https://www.globest.com/2022/03/31/supply-chain-disruption-accelerates-digital-transformation/?slreturn=20221110180619
28. https://stripe.com
29. https://www.fastcompany.com/90719976/stripe-climate-innovative-carbon-removal

30. https://stripe.com/newsroom/news/fall-21-carbon-removal-purchases
31. https://climeworks.com/news/climeworks-launches-orca
32. https://www.fastcompany.com/90719976/stripe-climate-innovative-carbon-removal
33. https://www.cnbc.com/2022/06/28/why-companies-like-stripe-meta-and-alphabet-are-behind-carbon-removal.html
34. https://www.firstinsight.com/white-papers-posts/gen-z-influencing-all-generations-to-make-sustainability-first-purchasing-decisions
35. https://www.bloomberg.com/news/articles/2021-11-17/gen-z-has-360-billion-to-spend-trick-is-getting-them-to-buy?leadSource=uverify%20wall
36. https://www2.deloitte.com/content/dam/Deloitte/global/Documents/2021-deloitte-global-millennial-survey-report.pdf
37. https://www.firstinsight.com/white-papers-posts/gn-z-shoppers-demand-sustainability
38. https://www.kcl.ac.uk/policy-institute/assets/who-cares-about-climate-change.pdf
39. https://www.cnbc.com/2021/08/10/the-environment-is-gen-zs-no-1-concern-but-beware-of-greenwashing.html
40. https://www2.deloitte.com/content/dam/Deloitte/at/Documents/human-capital/at-gen-z-millennial-survey-2022.pdf
41. https://www.unilever.com/news/press-releases/2019/unilevers-purpose-led-brands-outperform.html#:~:text=In%202018%2C%20Unilever's%20Sustainable%20Living%20Brands%20grew%2069%25,Up%20%28toothpaste%29%2C%20Wheel%20%28laundry%29%2C%20Calve%20and%20Bango%20%28dressings%29%3B
42. https://www.fastcompany.com/90743143/gen-z-is-going-to-reinvent-the-supply-chain
43. https://startupsmagazine.co.uk/article-why-millennials-are-ultimate-investment-technology-industry
44. https://www.canva.com
45. https://www.fastcompany.com/90721894/canva-design-platform-most-innovative-companies
46. https://www.mksguide.com/canva-user-stats/
47. https://www.stockphotosecrets.com/stock-agency-insights/canva-stats.html
48. https://www.fastcompany.com/magazine/issue-249
49. https://www.canva.com/canva-for-nonprofits/sdg-resources/
50. https://www.canva.com/newsroom/news/
51. https://techcrunch.com/2018/05/23/50-tech-ceos-come-to-paris-to-talk-about-tech-for-good/
52. https://www.techforgood.co/international
53. https://www.timesofisrael.com/amid-market-downturn-israeli-tech-firms-raise-almost-10b-in-first-half-of-2022/
54. https://techfundingnews.com/drivenets-raises-262m-funding-for-cloud-networking-software/
55. https://kr-asia.com/asia-leads-innovation-in-global-travel-and-mobility-tech-sector-report-says
56. https://www.cnbc.com/2021/08/09/jungle-ventures-on-southeast-asia-tech-start-ups.html
57. https://www.cnbc.com/2021/12/02/softbank-backed-grab-begins-trading-after-completing-spac-merger.html
58. https://www.usnews.com/news/technology/articles/2022-03-24/exclusive-indonesias-goto-ipo-books-covered-to-raise-at-least-1-1-billion-sources#:~:text=March%2024%2C%202022%2C%20at%2011%3A11%20a.m.&text=SINGAPORE%20(Reuters)%20-GoTo%20Group,the%20situation%20said%20on%20Thursday.
59. https://www.worldfinance.com/markets/top-5-latin-american-tech-hubs
60. https://alter.vc/portfolio/cities/sao-paulo
61. https://www.nesta.org.uk/data-visualisation-and-interactive/european-digital-social-innovation-index/
62. https://www.fintechforgood.com/index.html
63. https://www.healrworld.com
64. https://vimeo.com/640814126
65. https://ethicalmarketingnews.com/healrworld-partners-with-mastercard-to-launch-first-ever-united-nations-sdg-focused-corporate-debit-card
66. https://landing.solfacil.com.br/
67. https://tracxn.com/d/companies/solfcil/__iYyhFS2BJbhL-1vhS-q33b1zWGyd0CaP4e2P--IOhd2w/funding-and-investors
68. https://labsnews.com/en/articles/business/brazilian-solfacil-snags-100-million-from-qed-to-boost-solar-energy/
69. https://landing.solfacil.com.br
70. https://www.neom.com/en-us
71. https://www.fortunebusinessinsights.com/industry-reports/carbon-capture-and-sequestration-market-100819
72. https://www.computerweekly.com/news/252526986/UK-climate-tech-startup-investment-doubles-in-2022
73. https://www.g9cm.com
74. https://www.fortunebusinessinsights.com/industry-reports/carbon-capture-and-sequestration-market-100819
75. https://knowledge.insead.edu/responsibility/responsible-ai-has-become-critical-business
76. https://www.un.org/techenvoy/
77. https://knowledge.insead.edu/operations/tech-good-needs-good-tech-approach
78. https://www.accenture.com/us-en/insights/artificial-intelligence/ai-maturity-and-transformation
79. https://www.oecd-ilibrary.org/science-and-technology/venture-capital-investments-in-artificial-intelligence_f97beae7-en;jsessionid=4kkU0D6i0DR1f2iBOOeBbVr7nqM9gOfQr5_ljdOl.ip-10-240-5-146
80. https://www.mckinsey.com/featured-insights/artificial-intelligence/notes-from-the-ai-frontier-modeling-the-impact-of-ai-on-the-world-economy
81. https://emarsonindia.com/wp-content/uploads/2020/02/Internet-of-Things.pdf
82. https://techgloble.com/samsung-6g-spectrum-whitepaper-explained/
83. https://research.samsung.com/news
84. https://news.samsung.com/global/samsung-unveils-6g-spectrum-white-paper-and-6g-research-findings
85. https://www.marketresearchfuture.com/reports/6g-market-10951
86. https://research.samsung.com/next-generation-communications
87. https://unctad.org/webflyer/impact-rapid-technological-change-sustainable-development
88. https://www.skillsoft.com
89. https://www.computerweekly.com/news/252509481/Three-quarters-of-global-IT-decision-makers-facing-skills-gaps
90. https://www.skillsoft.com/press-releases/skillsofts-global-knowledge-skills-and-salary-report-finds-three-in-four-it-departments-face-critical-skills-gaps
91. https://www.forbes.com/sites/jackkelly/2022/03/02/the-lack-of-digital-tech-talent-is-an-existential-threat-to-business-growth-and-innovation/?sh=17d1db517628
92. https://www.routledge.com/The-Trillion-Dollar-Shift/Hoek/p/book/9780815364313
93. https://www.routledge.com/The-Trillion-Dollar-Shift/Hoek/p/book/9780815364313
94. https://www.bankmycell.com/blog/how-many-phones-are-in-the-world#:~:text=How%20Many%20People%20Have%20Mobile%20Phones%20In%20The%20World%3F&text=In%202022%2C%20including%20both%20smart,the%20world%20cell%20phone%20owners.
95. https://www.weforum.org/agenda/2022/09/decentralized-finance-a-leapfrog-technology-for-the-unbanked/
96. https://defillama.com
97. https://dune.com/rchen8/defi-users-over-time